A Sussex Life

86 Not Out

Sidney Farenden

ISBN 1 898950 03 2

© Sidney Farenden and Susan Rowland 1994

All rights reserved.
No part of this publication may be reproduced in any form
or by any means, without permission from the publishers

Published by Susan Rowland
in association with Sidney Farenden

Printed by RPM Reprographics, Chichester, W. Sussex

Copies of this book, price £5.95 plus 55p p+p, are available from:
Sidney Farenden, 3 Deans Meadow, Barcombe, Nr Lewes, E. Sussex BN8 5DX
or
Susan Rowland, 7 Offham Village, Nr Lewes, E. Sussex BN7 3QA

I dedicate this book to
my three godchildren,
Stephen, Diane and David,
with my grateful thanks
for not allowing me to grow old

Thanks

To Wally and Jill Hope, who first suggested I should write my memoirs, and have encouraged and helped me to carry on to the end.

To Mrs Patricia Hill and Nigel, for looking after me for ten days of convalescence on my discharge from hospital, and whose lovely sun room provided me with the inspiration to write.

To Mr and Mrs John Keffer, who have encouraged me from the beginning, took my manuscript to London to get it typed and 'computerised', and to Rosalie Horner and her niece Fiona, who must have spent hours 'unravelling' my writing.

To Len and Janice Peacock who gave me such support during my three visits to hospital and have been such a tower of strength since.

To Mrs May Pratt, who allowed me to copy some of her old Barcombe photographs, and to Stewart Still, who did the copying for me.

To Susan Rowland, without whose help and advice the publication of this book might never have happened.

And the many friends who have encouraged me to continue writing, when I might have been tempted to 'pack it in'.

Foreword

That Sid Farenden is now Barcombe's oldest native son still living in the village is, of course, interesting, but the importance of his memoirs lies in how he has lived these eighty-six years. Certainly my life has been enriched by knowing him, as I daresay have the lives of many others.

His passion for cricket is obvious, and he writes with authority about every aspect of the game, having played it from boyhood until the age of sixty, after which his experience and knowledge proved invaluable as an umpire and latterly as scorer. Until recently he was President of the Barcombe Cricket Club. He reminisces about games played and the players, past and present. He now vicariously enjoys the successful sporting career of his godson, David Peacock.

However, his devotion to cricket has not hindered Sid's interest in other athletic activities. He has encouraged two generations of village young to participate in all sports, subscribing wholeheartedly to the Olympic ideal of healthy body and mind. He has promoted and supported the making of necessary playing fields and appropriate facilities.

But there are other fascinating facets of this exceptional man. For many years he was responsible for the men's wear department of Ballard's, the High Street shop, served on the Parish Council and was an applauded actor in the local dramatic society. As Sergeant Farenden he served in World War II in this country and abroad. From an early age he has been a keen gardener, and, when my wife and I bought our cottage several years ago, it was in that role he entered our lives. He has been an excellent and tolerant coach, counselling what grows best in this corner of Sussex, tempering impatience when results were not instantly visible and exemplifying his creed that a gardener must be a philosopher.

This is an extraordinary tale told by an extraordinary man.

John W. Keffer

Penance Pond, Barcombe
25 September 1994

No. 1 High Street, Barcombe is the cottage on the right of the picture

My Early Life

I arrived on January 27th, 1908, number eight of a family of nine, born to James and Mary Farenden at No. 1 High Street, Barcombe. Why it was called No.1 I will never know, for it was bang in the middle of a terrace block of six. Two up, two down, and an attic up top. But it was home, and for the seventy years and eight months I lived in it, a truly happy home. I suppose my earliest recollections were of starting school at the age of four. I still cannot fathom out how we were all taught to read and write before we even got there, but perhaps my memory hinges on the fact that we had elder brothers and sisters, and that birthday and Christmas presents until the age of school-leaving always took the form of books.

My first teachers were a couple of spinster sisters, Agnes and Margaret Beech, known as Aggie and Maggie, not very affectionately I might add. They only lived two doors down the road from me, and in school and out were continually quarrelling and wrangling. Aggie was the dominant personality and a real martinet. She treated poor Maggie like a child, and I remember once she made her stand in the corner with her back to the class. Standards two and three were under another oldish spinster, but a much different type. A very sweet old lady was Miss Atkins. She had a room in the cottage next door, so l saw quite a lot of her, and as a result I had to behave myself.

Soon after I started school, it must have been about 1915, the staff was joined by a young teacher, Miss Gertrude Welsh, a local girl just through her training, who later married Bernard Pullinger, an ex-service man, who if I remember rightly was considered a bit of a hero. He took on Handlye Farm, part of the Conyboro estate, but Gertie continued to teach (apart from a short lapse when her daughter Pat arrived) until her retirement in 1955. In my opinion she was a first class teacher, and although she ruled with a rod of iron (more than once I had a clip round the ear which left a lump from her ring), she always remained a highly respected teacher. I well remember years later delivering a telegram to the school, and having to walk through her class to the headmaster's room. It was just before her retirement, and she was teaching in exactly the same manner with the same grip on her class as when she taught me. Mr Moon was headmaster during my early years at school, but as he retired sometime during the first war years, I remember him only vaguely. I do know that he prided himself on the standard of handwriting produced by his pupils.

Two examples herewith:

No. 1: My eldest brother's handwriting at the age of eighty. He did remarkably well careerwise on the railways, retiring as the head of the school of instruction for clerical staff.

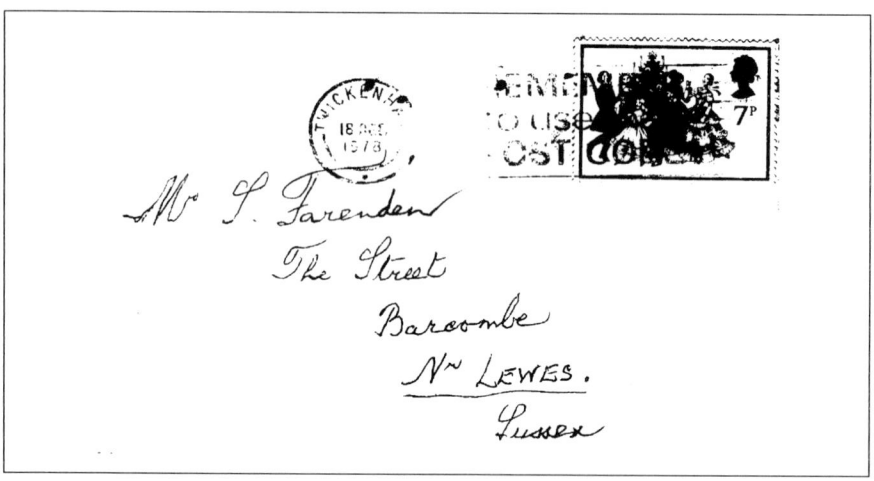

No. 2: A letter received from a very old friend of mine at the age of ninety. She also worked on the Railways and retired as head supervisor telelphones, Southern area. Miss Vi King, born at the Royal Oak, is still going strong at ninety-three.

More of school life later, but a little of home life that I have recollections of during this period. Father was porter signalman at Barcombe Station and a very busy man doing odd job gardening here, there and everywhere, even helping out at haymaking and harvesting for Harry Geering at Sewells Farm. He cultivated something like thirty rod of allotment gardens for himself, so we were never short of fresh fruit and vegetables at any season of the year. The family walks on a Sunday evening along the railway line between Barcombe and Newick were a very pleasant experience. Such a wealth of wildlife, fruit and flowers, much of which has now disappeared. A strict disciplinarian my father. At one of the Footpath Society meetings, as a member of the panel (subject: 'Old Barcombe') I was asked the following question: "As they had noticed in the school magazine that I had been 'School Captain' did this mean that I had been a good pupil?" I treated this as a leading question and gave no answer, but I do not mind revealing that the only time I received the cane at school, the news travelled home by means of my younger sister, and father gave me a hiding for getting it, so it didn't pay me to be other than 'good' or if I wasn't, to make sure I didn't get caught. A further example of father's discipline: an elder brother at the age of sixteen, whilst working at Barcombe Station, either got too fond of the girls, or was caught with his hand in the till, was shot off into the navy where he remained for the next twenty-five years. Father helped a little with our education, for he taught us all to play cribbage at a very early age, which meant we were good at maths.

His signal box at the station was always full of pot plants and bird cages. Many the bird he rescued with broken wings or legs from hitting the telegraph wires alongside the track. Mother was a quiet, hard-working woman, a wonderful mother and marvellous cook. She had to be to bring up nine healthy children in that house. No bathroom, outside toilet, only one fireplace, an old fashioned kitchen stove, but the food she turned out remains an out-of-this-world memory. One example: on Saturday mornings I had to purchase from the butchers half a pig's head for sixpence. Then she would spend the whole of Saturday afternoon making pork brawn, and I have never tasted brawn anything like it since. The larder was always well stocked with home-made jams, marmalade, preserves, pickles etc., even home-made wines. Her specialities were apple, which always sparkled like champagne and tasted much better, and dandelion. As I lived with mother in the old house until she died at the age of eighty-two, you will find several stories of her later on.

My memories of childhood during the first war years seem a little dim. We saw plenty of soldiers through the village as Maresfield Camp was the headquarters of a heavy gun unit, and groups on training exercises often came dashing through the High Street at a gallop. Very sturdy looking animals, the horses pulling the guns. We spent quite a bit of school time in late summer picking blackberries for the jam factory at Sheffield Park and collecting acorns to feed the pigs on the various farms. News came through of local men killed in action and there was much sadness in the community. Our next door neighbour, Mrs Peckham, lost both her sons within a few weeks of one another. My eldest brother, Ernest, spent most of the war years in Egypt and the Dardenelles area. Bill, the next brother at eighteen, was serving at sea on warships, but both had the luck and good fortune to survive.

I remember well the first motor car in the village, a red Rolls Royce owned by Miss Shenstone of Sutton Hall and most tenderly cared for by her chauffeur, Horace Verrall. Otherwise transport was all horse drawn, and the greatest excitement was caused by the milk floats dashing through the village to catch the 8.10 for London to transport milk from the local farms. It was as good as a chariot race to see Ben Paris of Church Farm and Jack Perkins of Burtenshaws' vying for the front place before reaching the station. I'm sure my father had to hold the train for them at times. Every morning I went down to Barcombe Place to purchase a pennyworth of skimmed milk. This could be anything between a quart and a half gallon, depending on the size of the can you took.

Games depended on the equipment you could invent or rake up. Special times of the year seemed to be set aside for certain games such as tops, marbles and hoops, and each activity would cease on a certain day. Marbles in particular seemed to wind up to a final on Good Friday morning between neighbouring villages. Tinsley Green in Surrey still carries on this tradition. It paid all the boys of my age group to become and remain friends with the Richards family, for old S. B. Richards (the local baker) was in the habit of attending all the home and farm sales in the district, and he would often pick up items of sports equipment such as cricket gear, perhaps an odd football, or a couple of hockey sticks which would not have been available to us otherwise.

Two great attractions for us boys were the local slaughter houses (two of them) on killing days (the bloodthirstyness of small boys) and the blacksmith's shop, now the local garage showrooms. Just writing of this brings back the aroma of burning hooves and the sound of the hammer on the anvil. To the rear of the blacksmith's was the wheelwright's shop, where one could see wagons, carts of all sizes and descriptions emerge under the capable and clever hands of Charles Chatfield.

Outings were few and far between. The local estates, Barcombe Place, Sutton Hall and Conyboro, each held an annual fete and flower show once a year and seemed to compete with each other as to the quality. The last big one at Barcombe Place was quite an elaborate affair. A brass band, an

The baker's shop and harness maker's, Barcombe High Street, early 1900s

Workers at the forge, early 1900s

athletic meeting attracting the Brighton Harriers, numerous sideshows and a grand exhibition of fruit, vegetables, preserves etc. Competitions galore: guess the weight of this, that and the other, finishing with dancing on the lawn until midnight. Barcombe Place also staged a Christmas Party for the Sunday School children, a Christmas tree with presents for all, a good tea and a type of pantomine show put on by the numerous young relations of the Grantham family, particularly the Richards and Austin families. The Ancient Order of Foresters Friendly Society, still going strong in the village (of which by the way I am still a trustee), always provided an outing to the local cinema in Lewes. I can still remember the very first film I saw. It was Rider Haggard's 'King Solomon's Mines'.

At about the age of nine I joined the church choir and received the magnificent sum of five shillings quarterly! What wealth! Even now every time I enter the parish church, such a feeling of peace and tranquility washes over me, bringing back memories of evensong with the old oil lamps flickering and the soothing sound of the organ, as we sang such hymns as 'Abide with Me' and my favourite 'The day Thou gavest, Lord, is ended'. Once a year the choirboys were treated to an outing to Brighton in charge of the choirmaster Mr Raban. Always a treat was a trip on the narrow gauge railway between the Palace Pier and Black Rock. A 'treat' for a nine-year-old boy was rarely different then and now.

One incident of youth I remember well. I was seven or eight and playing at chasing in and out of the windows of the cowstalls at Place Farm. Unfortunately I chose the wrong window for an exit and landed up to my armpits in liquid cow manure. I was rescued by means of a couple of planks, and travelled ungloriously through the village in a wheelbarrow pushed by Arthur Osmond. Mother was horrified and quickly got the copper going. Out came the tin bath and in I went, clothes and all.

The first money I earned was helping on a bread round with Stanley Richards on a Saturday, all day for sixpence. A paper round followed and just before Christmas a Saturday's beating for the shoot at either Sutton Hall or Conyboro. Two shillings and sixpence and a bully beef sandwich for lunch was not bad pay for this. One of the joys of childhood no longer available to the present generation was to take our tea to the nearest hayfield. I know as children we got great enjoyment from this. (Can you imagine taking your tea to the silage field today.)

In 1918 a new headmaster, Mr A. P. Bishop, arrived at the school, an event which I am sure had a very great influence on my life. To me he made school not just interesting but very enjoyable. One of the first things he introduced was a school magazine, issued two or three times a year. I have before me now a copy of the Peace Celebrations number of July 19th, 1919. The programme started at 9.30 am with a cricket match between servicemen and a Barcombe team. Many of the names on the score sheet which follows are merely memories, but some readers will find relatives and friends whom they can recall.

Service

J. Dudney	b Saunders	11
S. Allen	b Saunders	4
J. Cottington	c Cox b W. Dudney	1
C. Holloway	b Saunders	0
A. Dudney	c Frost b W. Dudney	3
B. Cornwell	b S. Cox	4
F. Heasman	c Saunders b Paris	5
G. Bodle	b Paris	4
A.P. Bishop	lbw Frost	27
C. Sayers	b Frost	16
J. Blackman	run out	2
T. Falconer	c Kenward b Raban	5
J. Funnell	b Raban	0
A. Frost	lbw Raban	0
F. Martin	c Saunders b Raban	5
G. Kemp	b Frost	3
E. Stevens	not out	0
	Extras	10
	Total	100

Barcombe

J. Perkins	c G. Bodle b J. Dudney	2
R. Rhodes	c Heasman b A. Dudney	0
S. Richards	b J. Dudney	5
G. Rhodes	b J. Dudney	0
W. Dudney	b A. Dudney	2
S. Cox	c G. Bodle b A. Dudney	32
B. Paris	b A. Dudney	16
J. Kenward	b A. Dudney	9
A. Saunders	c F. Heasman b A. Dudney	0
W. Hobden	not out	24
W. Raban	not out	9
	Extras	4
G. Frost	G. Bodle, F. Tapp	
F. Bodle	F. Cox, H. Stevenson	
A. Funnell	J. Stevens	
Did not bat		
	Total (for 9 wkts)	103

To continue the programme:

- 1:00 pm Dinner for all Soldiers and Sailors who served in the Great War
- 1:30 pm Fancy Dress Procession
- 2:30 pm Childrens Sports
- 4-5:30 pm Public Tea: Free to all residents in Barcombe Parish
- 5:30 pm Adult Sports
- 6:30 pm Concert, including singing competition for children; followed by dancing

A special word of praise must be given to George Farenden (my brother) for his solo so feelingly rendered; 'How beautiful are the feet of them that preach the gospel of peace'.

That first edition of the school magazine was one of many, and copies were regularly published until A. P. Bishop left Barcombe in 1931. To say he was an interesting teacher is a great understatement. Hobbies are far too numerous for all to be mentioned. Gardening and poultry keeping, bees, wireless at school, model railway, school cinema are but a few. A keen sportsman, and a first class cricketer himself, we benefited greatly from his enthusism for the game. Regular fixtures were arranged with the neighbouring villages of Newick, Chailey, Cooksbridge and Ringmer.

One memory of school cricket lingers. The game against Newick with both James and John Langridge in the opposition. On one occasion I remember the scorebook reading, caught John Langridge, bowled James Langridge eight times. James bowled his left arm round the wicket at the off stump, and John collected the catches at silly mid off. John and James went on to make names for themselves as professionals for Sussex and James skippered the side. He played for England against South Africa, West Indies and India. As youngsters they were greatly helped by the Newick schoolmaster Mr Oldacre and Mr Thomas Baden Powell, a cousin of the chief scout. The school game at Newick was always one to be remembered, played in those days on Baden Powell's ground, always a marquee erected, and a strawberry and cream tea. How could a small boy possibly forget that?

I remember when I first started playing we had to walk to these matches but later A.P. Bishop ran a Scott-Sociable. This was a peculiar vehicle. More like a motorcycle combination, covered, and which looked like a cross between a tortoise and a beetle. Four or five of us would climb into or on top of this machine and be dumped halfway and A.P. Bishop would turn around and meet the others. He was an excellent coach and our standard of performance improved greatly under his coaching. I often boast of taking five wickets in one over at Ringmer, but I'm sure I am rarely believed, so I cannot resist printing the following poem which extolled the virtues or otherwise of the school eleven of that year. It will also bring back memories of names that you knew many years ago.

Characters of the School Eleven
(By the School Poet)

Jack Poupart is our captain and a jolly good one too.
He plays with style, with cheery smile, of runs he's quite a few.
Behind the sticks he's full of tricks, and like old Strudwick, great.
He's a don with the gloves, it's a game he loves
Jack's our boy at any rate.

And <u>Farenden Sid</u>, great things 'tis he did
When we went to Ringmer that day
Our score it was poor, twenty-two and no more
Theirs was twenty for four, let me say.
But great shakes alive, you should have seen the next five
Whose wickets were taken - no kid
With five balls in one over, Oh! Barcombe's in clover
There's no doubt he's some bowler is Sid.

So that match was won by just one little run
And <u>Walls</u> put some strokes to the total.
He just dumped one beauty, my word it was fruity
It nearly went over the hotel.
We stood and admired, for the umpire was tired
With crying "Oh, why don't you hit 'em?"
His average is better, he'll be a run getter.
Well, walls are meant to climb not to sit on.

There's young <u>Welsh</u> known as Cherry, a very young berry
Who'll blossom before very long
Into a player quite tart, if he gets a good start.
For he can punch it he ain't very strong.
They say ducks like cherries, but that I don't know
But with this I'm sure he'll agree
That his pen he sucks, Cherry doesn't like ducks
But that's just between you and me.

Do you know <u>Charlie Smith</u>, known as Smiler by all,
But as Mulligatawny by many.
The soup was too bad, in the last match we had
For of runs he didn't get any.
However, he'll do, for to hear him say "OO-OO"
When the ball gently tickles his bail
Coupled on to his smile, it makes it worthwhile
To take him wherever we sail.

But of bowlers let's write, there's <u>Jack Osmond</u> as bright
As the rims on his bicycle wheels.
He's a terror with yorkers, some awful fine corkers
His analysis this truth reveals.
And <u>Faulconer</u>, too, when he gets on the 'goo'
Soon gets those old birds on the wing
Who come to the field, and think they can wield
And wave bats in the air till next spring.

Then the tail of our team, we've a very long tail
Composed of two layers of skin.

<u>Skinners</u> I should say, two brothers forsooth
Not noted for length of their shin.
However, that is they've had every chance
To show what the stuff is that's in 'em.
They've kept up their end, even made the bat bend
And that's just the stuff you should give 'em.

There was young <u>Jimmy Oakley</u> who stayed here some time
From some LCC school down in Brixton.
At bowling he tried, and between you and me
To be a bowler, his mind had been fixed on.
We're sorry he's gone; no doubt he is too.
And if I see him down by the 'Bon Marché'
I'll ask him who gave him the flowers he took back.
Say, aren't the girls at Barcombe recherchée?

We've a <u>Budd</u>, a very big bud, and he's blossoming too,
And will make a good cricketer soon.
He's coming on fast I hope it will last.
A lot of things come on in June.
And now I must end, this awful attempt
To sing of our deeds at the wicket.
Old football's arrived, to hide I've contrived
To next year, when I'll hail again CRICKET.

Lessons were made interesting, and a spirit of competition created between boys and girls by the introduction of spelling bees and mental arithmetic tests, and I'm sure our standard of spelling and maths improved considerably by these. The introduction of the motor car began to create changes in the village. Two brothers, Jack and Leslie Churches, started up a garage repair service and ran a taxi service with an American Packard car. The baker's horse-drawn vans became replaced by Ford vans, but Ballards, the grocers and general store, continued with the horse and van for some years after the end of the war.

A very eventful day during schooldays was the visit of Hobdens threshing machine to Mongers Farm. If I remember rightly this occurred early in the school summer holidays. We boys would arm ourselves with 'cudgels' collect any dogs available, and get ready for the war on the rats and mice. Once the thresher got going, the lower the stack got, the more plentiful the rats and mice, and what a noise. The rattle of the machinery, the yelping of the dogs, and the shouts from the gang of boys I can hear ringing in my ears to this day.

A traumatic time at home for, after a long illness, father passed away. His decline started with a fall from a truck, and he complained of his back for some time before getting medical advice and attention for it. Eventually he had to spend a couple of spells in hospital, and died in 1920 from spinal meningitis. Mother was heartbroken, for they were a very devoted couple. She retired to the back bedroom with her grief and remained there until after the funeral. She then went off to a brother of hers in Northamptonshire for a fortnight's rest while we were looked after by a spinster aunt from Eastbourne, a period my brother George, sister Rose and myself did not enjoy very much. A very religious lady, Aunt Kate, and many were the lectures we had to endure during this fortnight. Mother was welcomed back with open arms and much joy. George left school and started work at Bunney's nurseries, but could never get on with the foreman and soon left there to join the railway. His first appointment was to Mayfield, so he moved from home into lodgings and eventually married a Mayfield girl. They moved back to Barcombe Mills station and lived in the station house for thirty-five years until his retirement.

About this time a new horror comic made its appearance called the 'Wizard'. I managed to smuggle the first number into home, but mother discovered it and it very quickly found the fire. I also tried with number two, but mother also confiscated this!

"It's no good, Sid, you are not going to have this rag. If you want something more to read, I will get it for you!"

And so she placed an order for Arthur Mees' 'Children's Encyclopedia' at one shilling and three pence a fortnight which she could ill afford. Years later I passed these on to my eldest nephew and he in turn has passed them on to his eldest son. How wise my mother was.

My elder sister Edith was working at the local general store, Ballard's, and was there at the time I left school at Easter 1922. I hated leaving school, for, looking back, school had been as happy a time in my life as any. The fact that George had left home meant that I had to be responsible for the upkeep of the garden; and soon became interested enough to enter a few items, including the garden itself, in the last big flower show, of which I have made previous reference, and even walked off with one or two prizes.

And so it was out to work!

1922-1930

I suppose it was inevitable that I should start at Ballard's, the local General Stores. My sister, Edith was employed there at the time and I would guess that she arranged it. There was a very limited choice of employment, apart from gardening or farmwork, and as George was leaving home for the Railways, I was the last of the boys, and I suppose it was up to me to stay. My eldest brother, Ernest, doing very well on the clerical staff, did get me an interview and arrange an exam for me with London, Brighton and South Coast Railways (as it was in those days). Off I went up to London Bridge to sit for this exam with seventy five or so others. Evidently it was not the right time for taking on clerical staff, for of the seventy five, only five were offered employment and I was not one of the five. I am not sorry I didn't pass for my life would have been very different and I do not think nearly so interesting.

So it was errand boy at the local stores. My wages were five shillings a week, of which I gave mother three and bought my clothes out of the other two. Nowadays that takes a bit of believing. I had paper rounds to do and delivery of groceries, paraffin, etc. all over the village. I can still remember well the journey every Monday morning, loaded up with a large heavy basket of groceries on one arm and two gallons of paraffin on the other, I walked from the village to the old keeper's cottage beyond Curd's Farm, long since pulled down. I learned to ride a bicycle after a month or two and found plenty of journeys to keep me very busy outside in all winds and weather.

Leisure time was very limited, for I had to keep the garden going, but with the recreation ground so very handy to the garden, I was able to steal a few odd half hours or so for an impromptu game of cricket during the summer months. I was at the shop for four years and during this period my sister Edith left for a job in town and went to Purley to live with my eldest sister Margaret. Rose, the youngest, left school, and went into service. She also moved up to town, and I was left to look after mother, although at that time I think it was more of a case of mother looking after me.

It was at this time that Ballard's Stores were altered and enlarged considerably. A new shop complex was built on to cater for the men's side of the business selling men's clothes and accessories, cigarettes, tobacco, and confectionery. Mr Frank Ballard had taken over the management of the business from his father Mr John Ballard. Fresh from years in the RAF, he

Barcombe High Street, early 1900s. Our cottage is on the left opposite Ballard's

brought many new ideas and innovations with him but more of that later. When I reached eighteen years old, he told me that unfortunately he could not offer me a better position and suggested that I leave, and he would take me back into the business as soon as an opportunity arose. A job became available at Plumpton Green Post Office, which he persuaded me to take. Quite a journey every day in all winds and weather. Fortunately short cuts were available to a bicycle then, and the journey was considerably shortened by the route through the bridle path, across the main road, down Wickham Lane into East Chiltington, then through a farmyard at North Barns, entering Plumpton by the Sun Hotel. This journey has changed very little since 1926 when I first used it, apart from the bridle path, no longer a four foot wide gravel path and impassable during the winter months, and the closure of North Barns to all traffic.

Plumpton Green Post Office was owned by a Mr Albert Cheal and run by himself and his son Frank. Hours were long, but the counter work interesting. Monday 8am to 7pm, Tuesday ditto, Wednesday 8am to 1pm (half day), Thursday 8am to 7pm, Friday 8am to 8pm, Saturday 8am to 9pm. By the time I reached home and had a meal that was about it for the day. Everything came in bulk in those days and packaging the goods was a full time job. Tea, sugar, butter, margarine, lard, cheese, etc. I learned there how to cut up a whole side of bacon by hand, and can still hear the 'guvnors' voice behind me. "Keep your hand behind the knife Sid!" Although Frank did at long last persuade the 'guvnor' into buying a bacon slicing machine, he himself would never use it. I got on well with Frank and the rest of the staff. We were bakers as well as grocers and the smell of fresh bread through the shop still lingers in my memory. Then came my first opportunity to indulge in my love of cricket, for Frank was no mean performer and made many runs for Haywards Heath Wednesday. He had rigged up an enclosed concrete wicket in the chicken run at the back of the shop, and I often used to stay on for an hour after work, and practice with him.

Albert Cheal was a real old fashioned grocer, trained on the Pantiles at Tunbridge Wells. He was proud of the quality of the goods he sold. Here is a little story of him I will never tire of telling. One day a local farmer walked into the shop and greeted the 'guvnor' with this complaint.

"Haven't you got any better cheese than I have been getting from you lately. It all tastes like soap."

The 'guvnor' picked up the cheese taster and retired to the warehouse, pushed the taster into a bar of yellow soap and on returning offered the taster to the farmer with "Try this one."

After much spitting, spluttering and swearing from the farmer, and laughter from the 'guvnor', he calmly remarked,

"Now you know the difference in the taste of soap and cheese."

One other incident sticks in my memory. Treacle was sold loose from the barrel, and one night the bung decided to spring a leak, or someone left the tap on. However, the following morning the warehouse floor was covered by an inch of treacle, and this had seeped through the floor into the cellar below. What a mess! and what a job cleaning it!!

I got friendly with Jack Osmond during my four years at Plumpton. He was now working for his father Arthur who had started a small haulage business in the village. I would get up early on Sundays and travel with him in the old Ford lorry collecting milk from the surrounding farms and delivering into Brighton to the different dairies. This also meant an occasional visit to the various Picture Houses on Wednesdays, my half day, when we could afford it. Holidays had been few and far between, but one year I did get up to Purley for a week, and was able to watch some very good cricket, (always my first love in the way of sport) at Lords and the Oval. I saw such greats as Bradman, Jack Hobbs, Frank Woolley, Percy Chapman, Maurice Tate, Duleepsinghi and many others. Then came the opportunity for a real holiday. Jack Osmond had been ill, and his father Arthur decided to send him down to Somerset to recover and I was invited to go with him. Somerset was Arthur Osmond's home and as a young man he had worked on a farm on North Hill, Minehead lodging with Mrs Martin on Quay Street, which is where we arrived for this holiday after a long slow journey by train, finishing up on the branch line from Taunton to Minehead. We passed through little villages with attractive names such as Bishops Lideard, Norton Fitzwarren, Crowcombe, Blue Anchor and Dunster.

Mrs Martin was a remarkable lady. She lost her husband I believe in a fishing accident, leaving her with six children, the eldest boy only out to work, the other three boys and two girls still at school. At the time we arrived only one of the girls was still at school, and just the eldest boy was married and away on his own. A very lively home, always plenty of fun, with Beatrice, a little spitfire at thirteen, ruling the roost. I remember Jack and I fooling about locked her in our bedroom one morning. The next thing we knew, all our clothes and the suitcases came flying out of the bedroom window. We soon let her out! Minehead was a lovely place in those days, all the old familiar seaside attractions with life going on in such a leisurely fashion. To me anyway it was sheer enjoyment and I spent many holidays there up to and just after the second war years. Then in the 1950s Butlins arrived and ruined the place for me. The old cottage still remains in Quay Street occupied by Beatrice, the youngest daughter, who never married. I called in to see her four years ago, having lost touch over the past thirty five years or so, but she still remembered me and on opening the door remarked "Why it's Sid!". It was a delight to hear the old Somerset dialect again and to find the old cottage looking just the same. I always remembered the old dresser crammed full of china and it was still there with at least eight sets of jugs occupying pride of place as they did years ago. All the boys are now dead, leaving the two girls. Helen at eighty two, lives on the Porlock Road, still occupying the farm cottage she has lived in since marrying Jack who died a few years back. I asked her if she wasn't scared alone in this cottage for it lies back from the road quite a way.

"Oh no," she replied, "I still have Jack's gun behind the door."

"Ever used it?" I asked.

"Heavens no. I wouldn't know how."

Typical of the spirit of these two very independent ladies. I went to see them again the following day when Helen came in to shop, and enjoyed a good chat about old times. Minehead is an entirely different place with the arrival of Butlins. All the old business premises and hotels on The Avenue have disappeared to be replaced by Chinese takeaways, fish and chip shops, pizza parlours and bed and breakfast accommodation. I will never forget that first holiday in Minehead. I even remember arriving back at Lewes station late at night with exactly one shilling between us.

The following spring one of the girls at Ballard's, Esme Funnell, was married, and at last I was offered a position behind the counter. The business had become very go ahead for a village stores and had the reputation of supplying everything needed. One was never allowed to say "No" to a customer. Whatever the article the answer had to be "No, I'm sorry we haven't got it, but can we get it for you." Mother was very pleased to have me back home and in for regular meals instead of cutting sandwiches daily and I was more than pleased to get a regular lunch again.

The first summer back at Ballard's, in 1930, the opportunity arose for something more positive in the way of sport. Bob Richards and myself had managed to fall out with the local landlord of The Royal Oak and regularly used to walk out to the Cock at Ringmer. There we made many new friends, and made the acquaintance of the landlord, George Barrett, an ex 'Eastender' and quite a character. We were soon included in the circle of friends, who after turnout time on Sunday evenings were invited to walk down the front steps, around the corner to the back steps and inside for a bite of supper and a further drink. The local bobby usually joined us on these occasions. Here I met Harry Duffield, a Brighton auctioneer, who played cricket for Uckfield Wednesday, and I was invited to join them for a game. I played there regularly until the outbreak of war. A jolly club with only about fourteen or fifteen members. We were always together until about ten o'clock at night for a drink, perhaps a game of snooker and good company. Harry always brought me home but first made a late stop to pick up his wife at the Peacock Inn at Piltdown. Harry shared a farmhouse at Buckham Hill with a Mr Carey which he occupied at weekends. Betty, the landlady of the

Peacock always made us Welsh rarebit at midnight. How Harry's wife hated cricket!!

A hectic time to fit my cricket in, for I finished work at one o'clock, dashing across the road, and with a bag in one hand and a sandwich in the other, more dashing to Barcombe Mills Station to catch the 1.25 for Uckfield. I also managed to get in a spot of tennis at weekends. Winnie Holloway ran a tennis club on the Hamsey Road and at one time five grass courts were regularly in use. The club ran very successfully for several years attracting visiting members from Brighton. About this time it was very noticeable how transport was changing. More and more goods were delivered 'door to door' by lorries and vans. The old Ford van was very much in evidence, and a must for all the tradesmen. Passenger traffic continued to be fairly heavy in the late 1920s. Barcombe Mills and the River Ouse was quite an attraction on a Sunday and upwards of a thousand people would arrive. My brother George recorded the highest of over two thousand on one occasion.

In the mid 1920s I spent many Sunday mornings on the River Ouse in a punt. The stretch of river from the Anchor Inn to the falls at Isfield must be one of the most beautiful in the country. It was so unspoiled in those days, and very often I was the only human about, sharing this lovely countryside with the wildlife, so much more plentiful then, with no mink (escaped from captivity, or let out by animal rights activists) to destroy everything that moves.

Mother continued to live her quiet, peaceful life, an occasional whist drive her main enjoyment. She was quite wonderful to live with, never criticised any of my actions. I remember Nurse Rogers with whom she had become friendly saying to me,

"Sid, when I grow old, I would like to grow old as gracefully as your mother." What a compliment!

Also through going to Ringmer I made great friends of Dick Muddle (working at Ash Tree Garage), Bertie Thomas, whose father owned a smallholding just below the Cock Inn and Ern Lavender a builder and contractor's son who owned a business on the Uckfield Road. We must have become very good friends for I was asked to be best man at all of their weddings later on. (Why am I always the bridesmaid?)

1930-40

Mr Ballard continued to treat the business as more of a hobby. All the windows were dressed regularly, that meant at least six changes weekly. In 1930, the year I came back into the business a magazine called 'The Monthly Pictorial' became interested and published an article headlined 'The Selfridges of the Sussex Lanes'. It went into quite a bit of detail, describing how the shop was split into male and female sections, pointing out how men buying cigarettes were attracted to the display of menswear and anything to appeal to the masculine taste. Old John Ballard's motto of 'No, we haven't got it, but can we get it for you' was rigourously applied and deliveries by train and bus from the wholesale stores in Brighton were a regular daily event. It had photographs of the upstairs china, glass and hardware departments, an Aladdin's cave on its own, and praised the issue of the Ballard's Weekly News, a sheet circulated freely with suggestions regarding new bargains and eagerly awaited by the housewives of Barcombe.

Our rector during the 1920s and 1930s was the Rev. W. H. Farrar. A really good man. Often he would come into the shop to me, and leaning over the counter would whisper "Take a tin of Ovaltine to Mrs T. or a bottle of Bovril to Mrs J. and don't let them know where it came from." Yes he lived his religion did the Rev. Farrar.

Early in the 1930s I thought mother should have someone to help her in the house a couple of times a week. She had been suffering from high blood pressure and was not feeling too good at times. She was loath to do this, for her independent spirit was still very strong. However at last I won, and persuaded Mary Tickner to give her a hand a couple of days a week. They got on well together and became very firm friends.

Sometime in the 1930s I got the bonfire fever, a common complaint among the youth of the day, and influenced by Les Churches, a very keen bonfire boy, joined the Borough Bonfire Society and went mad on the fifth of November in the company of thousands of others. One year I even managed to get myself locked up. A policeman's hand on my shoulder at ten minutes to midnight for lighting a firework for someone else from my cigarette. This meant a very late arrival home (Dick Muddle with his Austin Swallow), eventually located in the parlour of the Prince of Wales. I tried to creep upstairs at three o'clock in the morning without waking mother but no luck. Suddenly, her voice, "Wherever have you been Sid?"

"Believe it or not mother, I have been locked up!" and at three o'clock

Ballard's Store, Barcombe High Street in 1930

A picture of myself behind the counter in the grocery department, 1930

The glass, china and hardware showroom at Ballard's Store, 1930 in the morning, seventy years old, mother burst out laughing and said,

"Serves you right."

Such was her sense of humour. We managed to start bonfire fever going in Barcombe about this time, very successfully for it is still going strongly today.

In about 1930 the Men's Club found themselves in financial difficulties and Leslie Churches, Bob Richards and myself were elected as a sub committee to raise funds to get us out of trouble. Among other activities we ran a 'Bachelor's Dance'. Leslie had heard of a new dance band just started up in Hastings and agreed to provide transport for them in the Packard taxi. The dance was by invitation only and we sent out 120 invites. We had the use of the men's clubroom for cloaks and refreshments. You may wonder what was so unusual about this dance, but when I tell you the name of the musicians 'Frank Chacksfield and his Band' and that we hired the four young men for four guineas, you will realize what an event this turned out to be. During the 1950s and 1960s, you would be paying more like £4,000 to engage this band.

It was in 1933 when I was laid low with phlebitis thrombosis. Five weeks in bed without putting my foot to the ground, and at the end of that to be told there was to be no more strenuous sport, no more dancing, and the support of bandages for the rest of my life. Depression wasn't the word for it. For twelve months I endured the mental agony, then went back to my doctor.

"Is there nothing you can do? Must I resign myself to a life like this?"

"Sorry, I cannot advise an operation of any kind. The risk is too great."

And so I decided to take matters into my own hands. I started playing cricket again, and in fact returned to my old way of life entirely, except that I did continue to wear bandages as support. How right I was for the treatment now for circulation complaints is exercise and more exercise. In any case it was the correct diagnosis and treatment for me, for it wasn't long before I had a five year spell in the army, passing a PT Instructor's course, running the hundred yards for the Regiment, and even had my medical category upgraded.

I played cricket until I was sixty, then twenty years of umpiring and have continued to score for the game I love.

I carried on playing cricket for Uckfield Wednesday until early 1940. The final game at Haywards Heath was interrupted four times by air raid sirens and as I left there in a hurry with a size six pair of cricket boots, and I take a size eleven, it was the end of my cricket until after the war.

The day war was declared, I was serving in the ARP while awaiting my call up, which I knew was inevitable. Air Raid Sirens at 11 am and I had to dash up to the command post at the Royal Oak. I told mother to stay in the house until I got back, or to go next door to the neighbour. Half hour later, with nothing happening, I ran back home to make sure she was all right. No mother in the house, no mother next door with the neighbour, and where do I find her! In the garden picking beans! No use grumbling at her with,

"I thought I told you to stay in the house."

Her reply! "You will want your dinner just the same, won't you?"

While in the ARP, a month or so before my call up into the army, we had a night air raid in which many many incendiaries were dropped all around the village. Mother woke me about 3am.

"Sid, quick, there are fires everywhere."

On looking out of the back window, I saw that Sewells Farm seemed to be surrounded by flames. Quickly dressing I dashed downstairs. Mother had my wellingtons all ready, plus my long handled shovel and my bicycle by the front gate. On the way over the only person I saw was old Mr Dean, waiting at the top gate, which he opened for me. I quickly dealt with all the incendiaries near any of the stacks, and as there seemed no danger of anything catching alight I returned to make my report. On the way back I met the fire engine just leaving the village. Red tape, for they were unable to get operational until receiving orders from HQ.

My call up papers came at last. November 1940. Now, what to do about mother. I approached George at Barcombe Mills. Yes, he was only too willing to have her, if she would come. She solved the problem most emphatically with,

"It's no use you trying to move me, I'm staying here."

And this before we even had a chance to suggest any alternative. However the problem resolved itself, for my youngest sisters husband was posted to Burma, so they decided to shut up house, store the furniture, and Rose came home to stay with mother for the duration.

Barcombe Station in 1910

Level crossing, Barcombe Mills

1940-1945

November 1940. And so off into the army. I met up with one or two obviously bound the same way at Brighton Station, then on to Blandford in Dorset. Age group thirty two! Twelve hundred in the draft! Bewilderment, the emotion foremost, and for the first few days I felt like a real fish out of water. Slowly I began to realize that my IQ was well above the average for my age group which did wonders for my ego. Training drills, PT lectures, I'm sure I trod on every inch of that square.

There was one particularly amusing episode which made me feel about one inch high. Pay parade on the square, second week. I heard the name Farenden and stepped smartly up to the pay table. A little second lieutenant, no more than twenty years old, eyed me up and down and then barked,

"And how long have you been Sergeant Farenden?"

I crept away with my tail between my legs, but looked up my namesake a day or two later. I discovered he was a training sergeant in B Battery and was a second cousin of mine. My brother, the naval one, had met up with him a few years ago in Portsmouth. Small world!

My ego received a further boost when I was one of eighteen chosen from twelve hundred men as NCO potential, and left Blandford as a lance bombardier. I said a thank you to my training sergeant, a Scotsman, who simply replied,

"Don't thank me laddie, you've only yourself to thank."

And so it was out on detachment as a cluster searchlight unit, about forty of us, with two sergeants (ex-territorial army) and three junior NCOs. We were dumped on a Sunday afternoon about halfway between Buckingham and Bicester. We just saw the site before dark. One large field with huts in sections scattered all over the place, with not a single one erected. We spent the first night, and several after, in a huge tithe barn, an exact replica of the one at Court House, except both doors were missing. Food was supposed to arrive before us but no sign of it. We heard afterwards that they didn't find the site until Monday afternoon.

The sergeants were useless. One of them thought, talked and lived for nothing else but sex, and the other was so ignorant, I had to write his letters home to his wife for him. They hadn't a clue how to deal with a situation such as this, so I collected the other two junior NCOs and a couple of ORs and we went on the scrounge. We returned about 8pm with loaves of bread, pots of jam, butter, cheese and pickles of all sorts. We had knocked up the local pub, never open on Sundays, pooled our resources and bought a couple of crates of beer. We found an old boiler, the sort they used for boiling up pigs' swill and at least got some hot water going for the morning. No fun shaving from the brook with icicles hanging from the bushes. The next two weeks it was slog, slog, slog, getting those huts up, but we soon had at least enough accommodation erected for sleeping and cooking. Equipment had to be in operation by the first night, but that we managed to do. Sometime during the second week, a car pulled up at the gate with a lady wishing to speak to the sergeant in charge. Neither of the sergeants would go and talk to her, so the task fell to yours truly. She came from the nearest village, Newton Purcell, about a mile away, and was just enquiring if there was anything she and her friends could do for us. A forlorn hope I thought but I would give it a go.

"Any possible hope," I said, "of yourself and friends being able to supply baths for forty men, say once a fortnight?"

"I will see what I can do and be back later this afternoon."
She duly reappeared having found ten homes who would take four men once a week. So from Monday to Friday on a rota system, eight men were able to leave the site and get a bath. What a godsend! but I didn't get the credit for that.

I suppose we were there for about three months, then it was down to Cornwall on the cliffs above St. Ives for most of the summer. Back into the New Forest for the winter, then Salisbury Plain for a month or two. I was promoted to bombardier and in charge of a site for the first time, and then promotion to lance sergeant followed quite quickly.

Mother and I had a good arrangement about news, for we both used to write something every day and post once a week. All the time I was in the army and receiving her letters, I never once found a spelling mistake. On Salisbury Plain I took over from a bombardier who immediately we started talking said,

"You come from Sussex, Sarge!"

"How do you know that?"

"I was born in Lewes," was the reply "and I know the brogue."
His two brothers ran a butchers shop. He, himself ran the W. H. Smith's station bookstall at Leatherhead, and knew my eldest brother very well before the war, selling him his daily newspaper every day on his way up to Clapham Junction. To think we should meet on Salisbury Plain. What a small world.

A couple of humorous incidents occured there. Our water supply was a very deep well and as will happen where wells are concerned, we lost our last usable bucket. The nearest house was the local policeman's, so I sent one of the boys down to ask him for his grabhooks.

"Go on, you're pulling my leg. What are grabhooks?"
However, he eventually went away and came back with a three pronged hook, quite small. They were all very sceptical, and even I was not very optimistic about the end result. But as we had a well at home and it had worked for me there, sometimes after a couple of hours fishing, I was at least hopeful. The very first time I put the hooks down, I hooked the bucket! They all thought I was a magician.

Town lads were funny at times, at least I found them so, coming from the country. One moonlight night, the sentry came and woke me at three o'clock in the morning with,

"Sarge, there's a most peculiar noise down at the command post, sounds like someone snoring, but I can't find a thing and its just like daylight out."

I knew what it was but also knew he wouldn't believe me unless I could prove it to him. When we got to the command post, I said,

"It's an owl, up in the oak tree there."

"Rubbish," he said. "Owls don't make a noise like that, they hoot."
So I picked up a stone, threw it up in the tree, and out flew a lovely big barn owl.

"There's your drunken snorer," I said, and went back to bed.

Another night, and this time it was 'bells'.

"Sheep," I said.

"But we haven't seen sheep since we have been here, and that's weeks."

"You will in the morning," I said.
And next morning there were hundreds and hundreds of them surrounding the site.

Changes once more, and the whole of the regiment was sent back to Sussex, Brede Place, near Hasting, for a complete sort out. All A1 and A2 personnel were to change to Bofors guns, while B category were to be transferred to Pioneer Corps. I arranged a hurried interview with my CO requesting co-operation from the MO. When I saw the MO I told him point blank that I wanted to be upgraded to A2 category.

"Never been asked to do anything like this before."
An examination followed, and as a result he said,

"I'll do it for your sauce!"
So I remained with the unit and went into training with Bofors guns.

Brede Place was a journey back into the dark ages. The villagers were convinced the place was haunted and wouldn't go near it after dark. Even when unoccupied they swore that lights suddenly appeared all over the house. To make matters more interesting, a previous owner, a Mrs Clare Sheridan (a cousin of Winston Churchill) came and gave us a talk on the ghosts that haunt the place (three of them). Number one was a servant girl, Mary, who haunted the grounds (one of the young lords of the house 'did her wrong') and Mrs Sheridan, when riding her horse through the grounds, often had the gates opened and closed after her by 'Mary'. Number two was a most unpleasant personage, who haunted one of the main rooms. This one was never seen, but a very cold, chilly atmosphere was felt by anyone entering the room. Number three took the form of singing and the smell of burning incense coming from the chapel at certain times.

When acting as guard commander, I often wandered down into the chapel. The big old oak door used to swing open on its own sometimes, scaring the daylights out of the guards, but my only experience of the supernatural was rather weird. I was on guard command one night when two of my lads reported in late after an evening in Hastings. It was a dark snowy night and after getting off the bus, they somehow missed the drive entrance to the house. On hearing someone approaching from the other direction they waited to enquire the way. This happened to be quite a youngish woman, who said,

"Oh, I'm going part of the way so I will show you."

And she joins them walking down the driveway. There was a five barred gate at the end of the drive with the house no more than a hundred yards away, and the woman suddenly disappeared. On arrival at the guardhouse, both lads were as white as sheets and firmly believed they had been accompanied by 'Mary'. I tell this story often. As there was snow on the ground I picked up a torch and went back to the gate, hoping to find three sets of footprints in the snow. No such luck, there were only the two. However when repeating this story as a Christmas 'ghostie', I do invent that third set for extra atmosphere!

Then the rumours started as to where we were to be stationed. I was made up to full sergeant (unpaid) and in charge of a gun detachment of ten to twelve men. When the eventual posting came through I was very disappointed, for it was Chatham Dockyard (no place for a country boy, born and bred). I hurriedly saw my CO.

"Is there no site outside the docks?" I asked. "I shall die of claustrophobia shut up in there."

"There is one site outside," he said, "Bang in the middle of some allotments behind Gillingham Station. All you have there is the gun. You have to build your own gun emplacement and command post, but a house has been commandeered for your accommodation."

"That will do me," I said, "That's a challenge I gratefully accept. I believe I would go mad if I had to stay in the dockyard area for long."

Once again it was hard slog, but I had a good lot of lads and it all took shape very quickly. The house was OK apart from being a bit cramped and

A picture of myself in army uniform taken whilst I was in Belgium

View from the railway bridge at Barcombe Station

as an added bonus my cook was an ex-Brighton hotel chef. The food was really good here for we were under the navy for rations and amongst other goodies a four pound corner of gammon ham used to arrive once a week, and cooked by our chef that was a real luxury. We saw little in the way of action here but we did manage to let off a few rounds at a Heinkel! He turned away from our direction without unloading and was brought down by the heavier guns before reaching the coast.

My bombardier, Dickie Dunne, was quite a comedian and could sing a jolly good song. I also had on site a professional drummer, Jackie Jackson, and he could certainly rattle the sticks. He and Dickie often used to entertain the locals at the nearest pub and became very popular.

Our site here was chosen for a visit by the CIC Home Defence General Sir Frederick Pile. He was very impressed with the set up and asked if I was interested in a commission. I replied that as I had no financial means other than my army pay, and some of that went home to support mother, I couldn't afford to live as an officer. He understood and said if my circumstances changed, to apply through my CO and he would see that I got through.

I nearly lost my Brighton chef here, for one day my Battery CO arrived just as we were having tea. I had managed to purchase cheap from the shop while on leave a couple of large meat platters, and the chef always cut up bread and butter on to the platters, rather than just dump the lot on the table for the troops to help themselves.

"I can make the butter go much further this way," he said "And it gives me a little extra to cook with."

When the CO saw this, he turned to the Sergeant Major and remarked,

"Why, we don't have tea served up like this in the officers' mess!"

A couple of days later my cook was transferred to Battery Headquarters. He was furious, and so was I!

"I won't stay there," he said "I'll make myself such a bloody nuisance they will be pleased to get rid of me."

And that's what happened. Ten days later he was back.

The time at Gillingham was easily the most pleasant I spent in the army. We got on well with the locals and at last I got paid for my sergeant's stripes! But all good things come to an end and our next move was just the opposite. The Isle of Grain (a huge oil refinery now, but vastly different then). Open marsh land intersected by dykes, flocks of sheep and miles of emptiness. It was interesting to me for it housed abundant wildlife, in particular ducks and geese of all breeds. We had a shepherd who lived practically on the site, and he had a marvellous dog, Bess, deaf as a post but could she handle sheep. Every twenty yards or so she would look back at Sid (my namesake) the shepherd, and just a movement of hand or arms would send her on her way. But was it cold there during the winter months. Those north easters direct off the North Sea were enough to freeze your bonemarrow.

Sid the shepherd was soon on good friendly terms with all the boys and as he lived alone and looked after himself entirely we were in the habit of providing him with dinner daily. I had lost my Brighton chef. He could not face the wide open spaces of Grain and applied for a posting back to town. We also missed our navy rations for we were back under the army again. It was early spring when we took over here and our shepherd knew where to find the shelducks' eggs, which were very plentiful here, and he would turn up with a batch quite regularly, always with enough for one each for the entire site.

I seem to remember very little about leave during this period of army life and my old friends just disappeared. Bertie Thomas had joined up immediately and on his first leave contacted me with,

"Just the man I wanted to see. I'm getting married on Wednesday and I want you to be my best man."

Poor Bert was one of the unlucky ones for although he managed to escape at Dunkirk, he contacted some obscure liver disease which left him a complete invalid and he died just as the war ended.

Dick Muddle also married before my call up and again I officiated as best man. I'm not likely to forget that event, for there was Dick and I patiently waiting at Malling Church. The bride had arrived but no parson. He was eventually located playing golf up on the hill and was hurriedly fetched to perform the ceremony. Dick completely disappeared from then on and I have never been able to find out anything about him from that time. Ern Lavender had gone into the navy but I saw nothing of him until after the end of hostilities.

I made a big mistake here for the time came for a change and as this meant going back to the dockyard, I elected to stay on Grain for another session. Unfortunately I lost my detachment and my relationship with the new batch was not a happy one. I think they hated the wide open spaces to a man, and I found them quite difficult to handle.

On top of that suddenly the V1s (pilotless aircraft known as Doodle Bugs) started arriving and this was a most frustrating period. In and out on stand-to night and day, and I myself spent three weeks without getting my clothes off. And all to no avail for the Bofor guns were just useless against them. No more than just a couple were brought down in our area. A few more by the heavier guns and our fighter planes were reasonably successful against them, but it wasn't until our troops on the other side of the channel began to overrun the sites that there was any respite from them.

In January 1945 the regiment was disbanded and we were posted in batches here, there and everywhere. I found myself in Belgium at a town called Dendermonde and quickly got myself posted to the stores (something I swore I would never do when I was first called up). The unit was a reinforcement holding unit and our job was to take seasoned troops back from the front line and pass them on for transfer to the war out east. In the meantime we were taking in batches of young eighteen year olds to reinforce the European front. The work was interesting and with my pre-war experience of handling clothing, etc. came very easy to me.

Something which had a lasting bearing on my later years happened to me here. At my first opportunity I made the trip to Brussels, only about half an hour's journey away. I had a pleasant afternoon, there were plenty of good clubs for NCOs and I returned by train later in the day. On the journey back a Belgian began to talk to me in English. He and his family had been evacuated to England during the first world war and he went to school in England. He was acting as interpreter to the US forces liaising with the local workforce. He lived in a small village, St. Gillis, just outside Dendermonde and on parting gave me his card and said if I liked to visit, he and his family would make me welcome.

The following Sunday afternoon I took a walk out to find the village of St. Gillis. It was no trouble at all, but it was a different matter trying to locate No. 101 Longdykstraat. Four times I tried passers-by but didn't find one who could speak a word of English and as I couldn't speak either French or Flemish I got nowhere. They tried in their way to give me directions but no luck. I was on the point of giving up when a chap came along on a bicycle. One more try, I thought, and that's it. I stopped him and showed him the card I had. Much to my amazement and good luck, he said in perfect English,

"Oh, that's my brother, I will take you there."

And so I met up with Emil and Emiline Moens and their two sons, Louis and Albert. Louis was on the point of joining the Belgian Army, where he made himself a career and retired many years ago, after forty years service. Albert was a fourteen year old, still at school. Emil was able to act as interpreter so we all managed to communicate at a reasonable level.

They always managed to find me something to eat when I turned up to see them, which I did at least twice a week, for I hated the sergeants' mess. Emiline was an expert with the waffle iron and she seemed able to make an appetizing soup from anything. The two evenings I spent with them gave me the opportunity to sit quietly and write my letters home to mother.

One of my duties early on at Dendermonde was to march a squad of these young soldiers out from England to a cinema called the Roxy for film shows. Anything to keep them occupied. Attached to the Roxy was a cafe run by Georges and Suzanne Metal. Georges was one of the leaders of the resistance movement in this area during the German occupation. Suzanne and a friend of her's, Vicky, ran the cafe and I was in the habit of spending my time with them while the boys were watching the film. We became very good friends and they both spoke passable English. We remained firm friends long after the war ended, and whenever I visited Belgium, never missed renewing their acquaintance.

Emil and Emiline gave me a home from home for the last eight months of army life, and I was always so comfortable in their company and never once was allowed to feel an imposition. Albert and I got on very well together and tried to teach each other English and Flemish, but I never progressed very far.

And so ended the war with Germany. I do not remember as much as I should do of the three days and nights of celebrations in the main square of Dendermonde, but it was almost continuous eating, drinking and dancing, and I am sure there were times when I was very much under the weather.

As soon as things settled, demobilisation started for all the long serving personnel, mainly the old territorials. One of the first to go was the quarter master sergeant (he told me he was more scared of civvy street than he had ever been during his army life).

I was immediately offered the post of QM, which I accepted only on the condition that I would be paid for it from the day of my appointment on orders. I had less than a week to learn to use a typewriter, for it was the QM's job to make out the payrolls for all the different regiments in the battery. I had one or two very late nights but managed to master the job in time. The changes of personnel from one theatre of war to another became more intense and the stores were kept very busy.

My visits to the Moens family became more frequent and whenever it was possible for me to get away I was there.

I witnessed one very peculiar phenomenon during late summer of 1945. I had to cross a few fields to reach St. Gillis and I remember crossing a potato field on the Tuesday of one week, with all the foliage very green, and plenty of white flowers. Travelling the same route on the Friday, three days later and it was nothing but bare stalks. The whole field was covered with Colorado beetles and brilliant red grubs. No wonder they treat the finding of one of these beetles so seriously.

Albert and I became very firm friends and he obviously looked for my visits with delight. I was able to do the family a small service by finding them a few surplus items from the store.

And so my demob date drew nearer and I began to wonder how I would adjust to civvy street once more.

1945-1954

December 5th, 1945 and I arrived home in my demob suit, which didn't fit, with about three and a half stone of extra weight, accumulated during my five years of army life, which meant that the clothes I came back to were not much use either. But what bliss, to get back to my feather bed and mother's cooking. She was still in fine form and I had little hesitation in deciding to return to Ballard's to work and agreed to start back in the New Year.

Changes had naturally occurred, particularly where work was concerned, for sometime during the war years the Post Office had arrived at the shop in my department. Frank Ballard had been so busy during the war years. He became billeting officer for the village, and then joined up as a special constable.

He found the men's department more than he could cope with, so when Miss Lena Hollaway decided to retire from the top shop and the Post Office became available, he snapped it up on the condition that Esme Burgess, as she was then, came with it. This worked well enough for it meant that this side of the business was kept operational.

Strangely enough I can remember very little about that first Christmas of the demob. Ernie Lavender was home and I do remember that Christmas Eve we spent at the Peacock at Piltdown renewing old acquaintances from pre-war years, but I have no recollections of what I did with myself over the rest of the holiday. The shop hours had changed considerably. Half day was now on Saturday and hours of closure much more amenable. A difficult time to start with for everything was in short supply and we still had rationing to contend with. I immediately began to interest myself in local affairs, particularly sport. I attended an early meeting of the British Legion at which I was proposed as the new Chairman of the Branch. The gathering was very shocked when I turned it down flat, and even more shocked when I strongly criticised them for not having raised a war memorial fund. Most other villages around had made some effort in this direction but not Barcombe. Plenty of dances had been held for different fund raising efforts but for a local memorial fund, no!

I informed the meeting that my energies were to be centred on raising a war memorial fund for improvements to the recreation ground so sport could continue as soon as possible to make up for those five years without.

I soon found a willing band of helpers to rally round and managed to persuade Mr Norman Sparke, who had recently moved to Barcombe and was living at 'Attrees', before taking up residence at Panthill, to become our Chairman.

He was very keen on cricket, a member of the MCC, and a committee member of the Sussex County Cricket Club. We soon got a fund-raising scheme started and a magnificent gesture came from Mr W.W. Bunney, Snr. He offered £100 if we could find nine others to do the same. We could get no further than seven, but with this and numerous other donations our fund reached the £1,200 mark.

The owner of the recreation ground, Mr Ivor Grantham, on hearing of our efforts, paid me a visit with the suggestion that as this was the form the war memorial fund was to take, it was his intention to give the ground to the village with the Parish Council as Trustees. What a magnificent and valuable gift! Several of the older members of the village were keen on starting up a bowls club and with lots of volunteer help this soon began to take shape. The cricket club also got moving and particular mention must be made of Wally Tickner's efforts in this direction. He put in hours and hours of voluntary work and in a very short while we had the reputation of one of the best village grounds in Sussex. Mr Sparke became the president of both the cricket and bowls clubs and his interest and enthusiasm was of particular help.

Part of the fund had been used to provide a children's playground and to get the bowls club started. During the war years a wooden hut had been erected, the property of the army authorities. This building was on a three monthly lease and we approached them with the idea of purchase for use as a pavilion. The price quoted to us on enquiring was £400. This was more than we were prepared to pay but someone on the committee came up with the brilliant idea of giving them three months notice to quit and offering them £100. This they accepted and so we now had a pavilion.

To make up for the years of cricket we had missed, we wished to begin playing on Sundays which a few of the clubs around were starting to do. A special meeting was convened where opinions for and against were freely expressed. Mr Ivor Grantham, the donor of the ground, was present. His opinion was that he had no objection to Sunday cricket providing it did not interfere with the morning service. We have always respected his opinion and have never started a game before lunch. We had just recently had a new vicar, a Bishop Saunders, and on being asked his opinion, his reply was as follows,

"I have travelled all over the world as a missionary and have seen the way Sunday is celebrated in many countries and have come to this conclusion. It is my job to look after the Christians and let the Pagans look after themselves."

Mr Maw, a very keen cricketer and a very religious man was very much against but the ayes had it and we were on the way. A mower came up for sale at Hillside Nurseries for £60, a 3ft Dennis. The cricket club had no funds available to purchase this but I approached the owner and he agreed to let me have it on the 'never, never' and I ran a series of dances to try and raise the cash. Every time I arranged a dance it either rained hard, snowed, or managed a pea soup fog, and eventually it took me two winters to raise enough cash to pay for this mower. Wally Tickner, in the meantime had discovered a large Atco machine. The very devil to start, and even when it got going would throw you all over the place every time it hit a bump. Wally was the only one who could either start or handle it.

I made some new friends through the dances for a gang of four driven by Henry Guy from Hayleigh Farm, Streat, used to turn up regularly; Brian Banks, Ron Thomas, Frank Brown and later, on his release from the RAF, Dennis Emsley. Henry Guy didn't dance and rather than see him sitting out, I used to take him in home for a drink and we became very firm friends. Later on these lads came over regularly during the winter months on Sunday evenings for a game of solo whist, a drink at the local and a bite of supper.

In 1947 I took over as captain of the 1st XI at cricket. Very few clubs had got really going for I remember that we played Hassocks and Keymer four times that season. The ground was coming along quite well now and the bowls green began to develop. Wally Tickner was putting in many, many voluntary hours on the cricket square. Alan Stevens, Len Barrett and several others were also pulling their weight. I spent many hours behind that Dennis machine, slowly getting the outfield down to a reasonable condition. Many an evening I finished up just before dark with a sore backside from the hours spent trudging behind the mower.

Towards the end of the summer of 1947 I suddenly decided to fly over to Belgium for a four day trip just to see how my friends were faring in the immediate post-war period. They made much of me, and I was able to repay in some small way for their kindness to me. Albert was due to leave school the following year and I left behind some cash for him to come over to England for a holiday which he agreed to do.

The shop life was not easy to handle for everything was in short supply. Cigarettes, sweets, clothing, all on coupons and any improvements moving so slowly there was very little enjoyment to be had from the business side.

Ernie Lavender was home now from the navy, but we had drifted apart rather and although I saw quite a bit of him, our relationship was not as close as before the war. Eventually he got himself a girl or, I rather fancy, a girl got hold of him and didn't let go.

1948 was a very traumatic and sorrowful year for me. Dear mother passed away in March.

I had been into Brighton with Ernie Lavender and Wally Tickner to watch ice hockey and returned about 11pm to find mother unconscious in front of the fire. I managed to get hold of Wally to go and fetch Nurse Rogers, who quickly arrived. Between us we managed to get mother upstairs and the nurse took charge for the remainder of the night. The doctor confirmed the following morning that she had suffered a stroke and then began for me the worst two weeks I am sure I will ever spend in my life. It was heartbreaking to see her lying there so helpless. To begin with she was semi-conscious and every time she needed attention or wanted moving it had to be Sid, no one else would do.

Nurse Rogers was a great comfort to me, for she assured me it would be about a fortnight she could be lying there gradually getting weaker. And so she went, peacefully on Sunday evening, March 8th. The new vicar, Rev. Bill Webb, was called from his service at St. Francis and he arrived to say a prayer and give us a few words of comfort. A friendship between us arose from that day which survived until his death many years later.

And so ended a period of my life which can never be bettered for the relationship between my mother and myself was a very close and harmonious one. The whole family was present at the funeral and for all of us it was a very sorrowful occasion for she was greatly loved.

The family all agreed that if I wished to stay on in the house, the contents were mine and I quickly decided that is what I wanted to do.

I managed to get lunches out at different places to begin with. I had a spell at the Royal Oak enjoying Maisie Grantham's marvellous cooking, a period with Mrs Larkin and then with Mrs Tickner. But it never proved convenient to remain at one place for long and I finally decided to have a make-shift lunch and do my own cooking in the evening. After all, I had plenty of experience of mother's cooking (never getting to the stage of buying half a pig's head and making brawn, that must remain just a pleasant memory) and managed quite adequately.

I had electricity installed. This I had tried to get mother to have immediately I came home from the forces, but she would have none of it.

"I've had oil lamps all my life, and they will do me until I die." was her answer to my suggestion and nothing would move her.

Albert came over from Belgium in July which took my mind off my loss for a while. He stayed for three weeks and had taken the trouble to take a correspondence course in English. We became much closer, for I found we had much in common, and over the years we have known each other, this became more and more pronounced with the love of the countryside and simple things. We spent quite a few days of his stay on the river in a punt

A picture of my mother taken in 1939

Barcombe 1st XI, 1950

Back row; Cecil Ridley, Chas Seager, Peter Austin, David Jones, Mr N.L. Sparke, Sid Farenden, John Heaseman, Bert Turner (umpire). Front row; Tom Bodle, Jack Clarke, Len Barrett, Norman Coppard, Percy Blackford on that glorious unspoilt stretch from the Anchor Inn at Barcombe Mills to the falls at Isfield. He got to like cricket and would be quite content to sit and watch whenever I was playing. The holiday proved a great success for both of us and we have spent many more together since, over the years. We remain the greatest of friends but we do not see each other very often now and have to rely on a telephone conversation once a month.

Now to my first meeting with the RNVR cricket team on August Bank Holiday. I had opened the shop from 9am to 11am as usual for Bank Holiday mornings. Four bodies walked in looking as if they could be nothing else but Royal Naval Volunteer Reserves.
"I suppose its no use asking you for cigarettes?"
"Are you the RNVR Cricket team?" I asked.
"Yes, we are."
"Well, meet the captain of the Barcombe team,"
and out from under the counter came four packets of twenty Players. And so began a friendship lasting until this day.

This year's (1994) visitors brought only one of the 1948 team, Arthur Hensher. Rather sad, but we had so many memories to recall. I will never forget that first game; Barry Crabb was the RNVR skipper. A wonderful company chap off the field but crab by name and crab by nature when playing. I remember tossing for innings with him which he won. Then two or three minutes of prodding the pitch and looking at it from all angles with Wally Tickner looking on scowling. Then "The bxxxxxs had such a night last night, I'll make 'em field to get it out of their systems." I learned later that they had been thrown out of the hotel that morning, the landlord refusing to have any more of them. Over the years we have had some marvellous games with them and they always managed to rake up two or three really eccentric personalities.

An episode occurred in 1951 when a nephew of mine, Jack Carter, had approached the club wanting to bring a team down from Croydon to play us in a Sunday fixture. We fitted them in for a 2nd XI game, but he had insisted that I should play. I wonder if afterwards he wished he had not been so insistent for I scored 98 and we won easily. They have been down regularly many times since and have always proved a popular fixture.

In 1949 I flew over to Belgium again and Albert took me into the Ardennes, southern Belgium for one week. This part of the country is vastly different to the north where Albert lives. It is very densely populated in the north and just the opposite if you go far enough south. A trip into Luxembourg was very delightful and in later years we spent several holidays there. During the second week I remember Albert had got himself a small motor cycle but riding it over the cobblestone roads around his home, his front forks snapped and he finished the holiday with both arms in plaster.

About this time, I started visiting a young lady (not so young for she was about my age and I was turned forty at the time). It lasted about a twelve-month and then I discovered two things. Firstly, she was never going to become interested in cricket. Yes, she used to come along, bring her knitting and managed to look very bored and as I was sure cricket would play a very big part for the remainder of my life, it was bound to mean friction. Secondly, I suddenly discovered that I couldn't live with the sound of her voice for the rest of my life. I'm sure it would have been continuous nag and so I remained the complete bachelor. The man who never made the same mistake once.

1951 was the year which really put Barcombe on the map cricket wise. It was the year that the Sussex County Cricket Club formed a Welfare Association to organize the fund raising efforts for the players in their testimonial year. George Cox was the first of these and was allocated six games in which he could call on the Sussex players to support him. Mr Sparke managed to organize an extra game at Barcombe. I recall going down to the county ground at Hove with him to a meeting. Col Grimston was the Sussex County secretary at the time and he was very awkward about allocating this extra game at Barcombe. He informed George Cox that he would not be able to call on the Sussex players for this game. George replied that he had not intended to, and that he had asked the Derbyshire players who were at Eastbourne that weekend to turn out for him. And so this game was organized and what a success it turned out to be. A glorious day, the ground in immaculate condition and for Barcombe a really big crowd. I remember the secretary of the Welfare Association turned up with another of the committee and quickly decided there was nothing for them to do and they soon departed for a pre-lunch drink at the Royal Oak. The game duly got under way with naturally George Cox's XI batting first, and we did very well to take all ten wickets for 217 runs. A different matter when we batted for we were all out for 78. I opened with Dennis Redfern, and in Les Jackson's second over my middle stump went for a somersault. Not surprising as he was opening the bowling for England at the time. I found a chicken coop in my front garden later, to house my 'duck'. It was no doubt placed there by Cecil Ridley, so typical of his sense of humour. Club cricket on Sundays was shared between the 1st and 2nd XIs, playing on alternate Sundays. So once a fortnight I was free. I joined the Streat and Westmeston Club and very much enjoyed the games I played there with my Streat friends in such truly rural surroundings. I often met up with them on Saturday evenings and at Henry Guy's invitation spent the Saturday night with his family at Hayleigh Farm.

Things were picking up at the shop. Supplies were getting more plentiful which kept everyone busier and happier.

The number of cars in the village was on the increase and it was most noticeable how things were changing on the farms. Horses were fast being replaced by mechanical means and the young men were no longer resigned to work on the farm, many getting work away from the village. About this time, I got myself elected to the Parish Council and continued to serve in this capacity for the next twenty two years. It was frustrating work for all important decisions had to be referred to higher authority, namely the East Sussex District Council. Occasionally, with my knowledge of local affairs, I was able to be of some help, but mainly I felt it was a bit of a waste of time. I did enjoy battles with the Rector for Bill Webb and I had many arguments but this made no difference to our friendship. The Hon. Sylvia Fletcher-Moulton was in the chair in those days and often, during arguments with Bill, I would catch her eye and get a wink from her as much as to say, "Carry on! I'm enjoying this." She proved an excellent chair(person) for she was a very clever woman, as anyone who knew her would tell you. An amusing story I must tell you of the Hon. Sylvia about this time. She was a very busy person, serving on numerous committees and as chairman of magistrates at the County Court. She went dashing down to Barcombe Mills in her car one day just as my brother George was closing the gates.

"Oh George, I'm in an awful hurry, can't you possibly let me through?"

"Not if you were the Queen of England, ma'am." George replied.

At which she burst into laughter. She could be a bit overpowering at times, but I always got on very well with her and had many an interesting chat over the wall at Penance Pond, when she came out to exercise her dog.

Business was improving at the shop, particularly in the men's clothing and footwear department. To begin with I found Esme Burgess, as she was then (a year or two later she married Reg Blackford, the postman), such an easy person to work with. Her patience, understanding and help for the old people in particular at the Post Office was unbelievable and never once, all the years we worked together did we exchange a cross word. On her retirement after the change of ownership of the business, I know she was sorely missed, particularly by the old age pensioners.

I had found a wholesale firm in Brighton, W.R. Newcombe and Co. of Richmond Gardens who gave me an exceptional service for special orders. A telephone call for things like a special size in footwear or a shirt, sports jacket or trousers, and I could rely on delivery by train or bus the same afternoon.

We had taken up an agency for Timex Watches and over the years must have supplied half the village with these. I did all the buying for the hardware, china and glass department, supplies for which had eased considerably.

1952 was easily the year that had the greatest influence on my life, an influence that has lasted to the present day.

I had become very much involved with the Barcombe Football Club. Apart from taking on the treasurership, I had also a year or so previously been elected as vice chairman of the Lewes and District Football League. So winter Saturdays saw me running the line for either 1st or 2nd XIs or perhaps just as a supporter, but regularly involved in some way or other.

Thus it was I first met Len Peacock and from now on you will find it is as much his story as mine. An old Barnado's boy, his father having died when Len was about four, his mother evidently was unable to cope with a large family, and the two youngest were placed in the care of Dr Barnado's. Len never saw the inside of a Barnado's home, for which I had the greatest admiration, for we had one in Barcombe with a Miss Peterson as a very dedicated principal. No, Len had been immediately put out to foster parents and as a result didn't have a very settled childhood and no chance to make any sort of permanent home. By the time I first met him at the age of eighteen, the chip on his shoulder was very pronounced.

It was through football I got to know him for he quickly gained a permanent place in the first eleven. He always looked scruffy when he turned up to play; his kit looked as if it hadn't been washed and it was noticeable that even his wounds from previous games had not received proper attention. He was working at Mansfields, the motor repair service works in Lewes, and fortunately was able to get a midday canteen meal.

He had become friendly with Peter Grantham, son of the landlord of the Royal Oak, and they often went into Lewes to the cinema on a Saturday evening. I got Peter to bring him along to my place for a drink when they arrived off the last bus and slowly his story came out.

I decided then that I would try and do something for him and it was my intention to offer him a home with me for about three months to try and straighten him up, and then find him a decent lodging in the village, for I was far from satisfied with the home he was in at the time. I got legal advice through a solicitor friend and found that providing there was no court order against him, he was free at the age of eighteen to do as he pleased.

I wrote to Barnado's as to my intentions, and they sent a representative down to see me. He advised me strongly against taking this action, trying to put me off with the remark,

"We have had this boy in our care since he was four years old. He is just thoroughly dirty and nothing can be done about him."

I think this remark, more than anything else finally determined my actions. So I put it to him that if he would give a week's notice to his landlady, I was perfectly willing that he could share my home for a time, until I felt able to make other arrangements for him. He agreed to do this, and so he duly arrived. He had very little clothing fit to wear, no hairbrush, toothbrush, or anything else much. Mr Ballard agreed to let me have clothes for him at wholesale price, and I remember the remark he made on putting on his first real suit, "I feel like a king."

I informed Barnado's of my actions and received a very strongly worded letter back from them saying they could not condone the boy staying with me with no woman in the house. Very understandable, but not so the fact that they made no effort to check up on me, such as an approach to the local Rector, or the chairman of the Parish Council as to my suitability in taking this action. I spoke to Nurse Rogers, putting her in the picture as a friend whose advice I valued and her response was, "I think it most noble of you, Sid, but you are taking an awful risk."

So Barnado's simply washed their hands of him and took no further interest. He seemed to settle down fairly well. Naturally there were one or two difficult moments, but no more than I had expected. He was performing well on the football field and was chosen to play in a couple of representative games for the Lewes and District League. But I could not get close to him, and he was certainly not ready to leave me after three months. In fact it was six months before I heard him really laugh.

I recall one evening walking through the garden to the recreation ground and people passing in the lane calling out,

"Hello Sid, Hello Len." He turned to me and said,

"People are very different to me now, and seem to want to know me." Then, in a complete change of voice,

"But I suppose that's because I'm with you."

And that's how things were. Come the better weather, he spent quite a lot of time down at the 'Oilmills' helping the Browns out with the boats for hire so I didn't see a great deal of him at weekends, for I was always busy at cricket.

As things seemed to be working out reasonably well, I then decided to keep him until he had to do his National Service when he was nineteen in February. In fact, I persuaded him to sign on for three years in the RAF and carry on with his trade as a motor mechanic. I did wonder at the time if this was a wise move for I thought that away from a home he would gradually drift away, find other interests and disappear out of my life altogether. However, this was not to be, for once a month on his weekend off he would turn up (having come all the way from Shropshire where he was stationed) by some means or other, mostly by hitch hiking. He learned to drive and had no difficulty in passing his test and seemed to be enjoying forces life.

I did suggest to him that as he was stationed no great distance from his home town of Oldham, he should take the opportunity of trying to find his people one weekend. This at last he agreed to do, although the result was not quite what I expected. I will not go into details of what he found, in fact I know very little about it, for when I asked him about it I recall his remark, "Don't you ever ask me to go there again," and from that day to this he has never talked of his family. It is just a closed book to him.

1952 was also the year that brought back memories of schooldays, for Jim Langridge was the beneficiary of the Sussex Cricket Club Welfare Association. He had been a very regular player for the county and had captained the side for a few years, also representing England at test level. Again, the game was a huge success, attracting many spectators from neighbouring villages.

John Langridge, younger brother of Jim, was our visitor from the county this year, 1953, and another successful event. What a charming gentle man John is. I was in conversation with him by telephone a few nights ago and at the age of eighty four he still sounded the same and it was such a pleasure to hear his voice again.

I always thought he was most unfortunate never to represent England at test level, for apart from his excellent record as an opening bat, his fielding at first slip was second to none. But with Hobbs and Sutcliffe as England's openers at the time, his chance never came.

The following year, 1954, I was at a loose end about holidays. Albert, my Belgian friend, was now in the army doing his national service for three years, so my Belgium trip was off. I had always wanted to visit Scotland and with Len now able to drive, I thought this would be a good opportunity. I suggested this to him and he was quite excited at the idea, so I fixed my holidays when he would be on leave and hired a car.

Jack Osmond approached me, asking if I would take his son John along with us. I saw no objection as he would be a companion for Len, nearer his own age. We decided against booking up anywhere, just take pot luck with bed and breakfast accommodation. This worked very well and we had a very successful and enjoyable holiday. I well remember our last night, spent at a farmhouse just out of Gretna Green. The cows coming in for milking woke us at an unearthly hour, but what a breakfast. The inevitable Scottish porridge to start with, then a huge plate with three eggs, three rashers of bacon, fried Scottish pancakes - a huge plate of these on the side, plus mountains of bread and butter, and we were fortified for our journey home.

1954-1969

I had retired as captain of the 1st XI at cricket, changing roles with Len Barrett, who had been such a helpful vice-captain for the past seven years, and for the next four years this relationship continued to flourish successfully. We were not so lucky with our county representative fixture this year, Charlie Oakes benefit, as we were completely washed out. However, our president came to the rescue and gave up his fixture for the President's XI to be able to play this game for Charlie Oakes, and once again we were blessed with a perfect day, and again a very successful effort.

The 2nd XI were having a very good season with Stan Hobden as captain and Ray Carey as his vice-captain. Ernie Carey had taken up umpiring and was later very much in demand at a higher level with Sussex Martlets and then on a regular basis with the County 2nd XI. He also took over as chairman of the Club, a post which he successfully held for the next ten years.

The following year, 1955, was one of my best, performance-wise. Against the RNVR on August Bank Holiday I scored my second hundred for the club. 127 not out and one of the best innings I have ever played. Again, the county came along for a benefit game, Jim Wood this year. A very popular figure for his home village was Horsted Keynes. He had bowled his heart out for the county over a number of years. Later on, when I took to umpiring I met up with him at Ardingly College where he had carried on after he retired from the county, as groundsman and coach.

It was this year that the Barcombe Players started up and began producing plays twice a year with great success, which have continued to the present day. I think it was Mrs Kath Stevens whose enthusiasm started the Players off, for I believe she managed to get Rodney Millington interested. He was living at Penance Pond and was one of the directors of a casting agency called Spotlight. For the first year or so the Players concentrated on one act plays which proved very popular with the village audiences. With Rodney Millington producing the standard of performance was very high. I had always been keen on amateur dramatics and took a very active part for many years, until old age stepped in and my memory began to let me down.

I again took my holidays when Len was on leave and once more hired a car. We spent a week in the West Country, making Minehead our headquarters, staying at the Beachaven Hotel on The Avenue. In those days it was still a very select area, all small hotels, typical middle class accommodation. How different since Butlins arrived in the town. The last time I visited Minehead, The Avenue was all Chinese and Indian takeaways, fish and chip shops, pizza parlours, and bed and breakfast overnight stops. Our holidays were in May, a bit early in the year for good weather, and we got caught in a snowstorm on Exmoor, heavy rain on Dartmoor, and a pea soup fog when we visited Widdicombe in the Moor. However, we enjoyed ourselves and managed to get around sightseeing quite a bit.

A Sunday fixture at Streat and Westmeston. It was Henry Guy's 21st birthday and was his choice for celebrating this. Stan Hobden captained the side and through my close connections with the family I was invited to play. As a cricket match it was very successful but for myself a very sad occasion for Mrs Guy was very ill with cancer. She insisted that I should go to the house to see her and I realized that she had not long to live, but ill as she was she had insisted that this match should not be cancelled on her account. She died later in the year and it proved to be the beginning of the end for the Streat Club at Hayleigh Farm. Henry Guy senior went to pieces after his wife's death and followed her soon after. As they were only tenant farmers it meant selling up. Henry junior was the only child and he moved right away from the village, and the club had to find another venue which they did and continued to play under the old title of Streat and Westmeston at Middleton Manor, Westmeston, but the club was never the same again.

A busy time for the Parish Council. The railway from Culver Junction to East Grinstead was due for closure. Barcombe station was kept reasonably busy with passenger traffic into Lewes and Brighton. Not so, the stations up to East Grinstead, for these were mainly placed far from the villages, the main purpose of the line when installed was for the transport of milk from the farming community to town. We did all we could in the way of raising a petition but closure came in 1955. It was then discovered that the Transport Commission were under a statutory obligation to run four trains a day and the line was once more opened. This arrangement continued until a bill went through Parliament and it was 1958 before finally the last train left East Grinstead for Lewes. Quite an occasion for there were 870 passengers on board.

In 1956 Len finished his three years in the RAF. He found a job with a motor tyre firm in Lewes but soon left there and went on to collection and delivery of eggs for Stonegate. He started going steady with a girl from Plumpton, Janice Thomsett, and spent quite a lot of time there.

Cricket was going well and Jim Langridge received a further testimonial and brought a team along for another Sunday fixture. The RNVR game on

August Bank Holiday was a very memorable one. We had a full morning's play with the RNVR batting and at lunch the game was evenly poised. On returning from lunch at the Royal Oak, we had just reached the pavilion when a terrific storm of thunder and hail hit the ground with tremendous ferocity. It began with hailstones the size of walnuts and then developed into a terrific downpour. The ground became covered with inches of hailstones and piled up in front of the pavilion doors at least a couple of feet high. What was so unusual about this storm was that a mile outside the village in all directions it was perfectly clear, but exactly the same thing happened at both Tunbridge Wells and Arundel. There are pictures of this event in the Womens' Institute Barcombe book, which are very interesting. There was no further play at cricket for there were still hailstones on the ground the following day. We adjourned to the Royal Oak in the afternoon and I walked over with Dr Jim Lewis, the RNVR president. We had to make our way through my garden as the lane was under water. It was an amazing sight for the tomato and potato plants were stripped of leaves, marrows looked as though they had been machine gunned, and the smell of onions, battered by the hail, was enough to make your eyes water.

"Is this your garden, Sid?" Jim asked.

On my reply of "Yes", he said "Whatever are you going to do with it"

"Start planning for next year," I replied to which he remarked,

"What a philosopher."

On reaching the Royal Oak a card game was already in progress. I asked to join in and Dr Lewis said,

"That will cost you five shillings."

I had no change and gave him a £1 note which he promptly tore into four, placing one piece in the kitty. Slippery Sam was the name of the game and in no time at all my £1 note had finished up in twenty seven pieces. However, I won the kitty and eventually stuck them all together. What an evening we had, drowning our sorrows at loss of a game of cricket, but what good company the RNVR boys were. I am sure they will never forget that day.

1957 and sad and worrying days at the shop for the governor, Frank Ballard died. He was greatly missed by all the staff for he had always been a caring and understanding employer. He was also a loss to the village for he had been much involved with parish affairs since the end of the first world war. Mrs Ballard carried on as best she could until the youngest daughter, Doreen, returned from Australia where she had been for the past few years with her sailor husband. She took over the reins of management on her return but had to rely heavily on the staff. Her husband on leaving the navy took up a job on a weather ship somewhere among the Scottish

The Sports Pavilion after the hailstorm in 1956

Islands and was away for quite long periods.

Albert, my Belgian friend, was now married but I renewed my visits to him this year and we spent a lovely holiday together in the Black Forest area of Germany. His wife Jose is a charming girl and we had much fun trying to understand each other. Over the years she has managed to pick up English far better than I have either French or Flemish (the Englishman's arrogance expecting everyone should learn our language, rather than we learn theirs).

Len was courting very strongly and it would not surprise me to learn of his engagement.

1958 and the first season since 1950 that we had no visit from the county at cricket. The welfare committee had decided that they could get much larger gates and a great deal more revenue by staging these games at towns rather than villages, and as most of the county sides were prepared to accommodate them that is where they went. We quite understood this and were very proud to have been of assistance to them right from the beginning. The cricket club suffered a severe loss by the sudden death of Mr A.J. Bishop who had served the club so well as both secretary and treasurer for some years. He had handed over the secretary's job to Charles Seager but was still very active as our treasurer and as I was assistant treasurer, I had to take over immediately. Fortunately the books were in very good order and I had no difficulty in stepping into his shoes.

Albert and Jose came over this year, Albert bringing his car. I planned a surprise for them by taking the car and themselves down to Newhaven, putting them on the sleeper train to Scotland, not letting them know where we were going. The last twice I had been over to Belgium, Albert had met me at the airport, dumped my bags in the car and set off with myself never knowing where we were going to spend the holidays, so I was giving him the same treatment. We had a wonderful sightseeing holiday making our headquarters at Pitlockry in the Trossacks and returning leisurely back to Sussex via the Lake District.

Len did get engaged to Janice this year and planned to get married the following May. He had again changed his job, taken on by the Buxted Chicken Company, raising broiler chicken for the retail trade. This meant accommodation with the job and I am sure he had this in mind for he had little chance of getting a rented house, council property being very difficult to come by.

1959 and Len was married in May. They spent their honeymoon in Paignton and travelled around the West Country sightseeing. On their return they started married life at Crowborough and spent the whole of the summer living in a caravan on the site of the chicken farm while a bungalow was being built for them. I remember it was a glorious summer and a lovely spot to be out on Ashdown Forest. I wasn't able to spend much time with them but I enjoyed very much my occasional visits and nearly always we set up a deer when walking through the woods; they were quite plentiful in that area. The bungalow was finished for them by the end of the summer and although isolated was a very pleasant spot. I visited them more often once the cricket season had ended and spent my time there, planning and making a garden for them. Being virgin soil everything seemed to grow well and by the following year, between us, we had made reasonable progress.

The Barcombe Players produced their first three act play and I had one of the leading parts. Rodney Millington produced and acted in 'If Four Walls Told' and it was a huge success. I had taken over as captain of the 2nd XI at cricket this year and was having some very enjoyable games with them. Again a trip to Belgium for holidays and this year on arrival at Brussels Airport we travelled on at once into Luxembourg. Albert had booked at a little village called Born, at the Trout Inn. A very pleasant spot with a small trout stream running by and surrounded by vineyards. I remember this spot particularly well for opposite the Inn was a small village hall. I think most of the village population played in the local brass band for every night there was a rehearsal in the hall. Quite entertaining to begin with but by the end of the week it became a little monotonous, for they continuously rehearsed the same piece of music, I guess for some competition.

Into the sixties and an enthusiastic start by the Barcombe Players. Rodney Millington was away and unable to undertake the spring production and it was decided to ask Lionel Green of the Lewes Little Theatre if he would be willing to fill the gap. He agreed to do so and decided to put on 'The Farmer's Wife', Eden Philpott's play set in Devon. A very ambitious choice for it meant scene changes and a very large cast for our small stage. I was chosen to play the lead, Farmer Samuel Sweetland, and how I enjoyed it. I knew the play well and I could manage a bit of 'Sussex brogue', so very similar to the Devon dialect it was written for. I enjoyed every minute of rehearsals and performances and it turned out a huge success with full houses on all three nights. An excellent write up in the local press and for myself a very satisfying experience.

Len and Janice started a family, baby Stephen arriving on the last day of April. A lovely contented baby boy who I quickly grew very fond of. The garden at Crowborough was progressing very well and we had quite a large area fenced and walled off, and cultivated. I was visiting once a fortnight regularly for I was no longer going to Streat for cricket now that

Henry Guy had left the district, and spent most of the day in the garden.

There was another sad loss to the cricket club, for our president, Norman Sparke, had passed away. A couple of years back he had broken his neck in the hunting field and had worn a surgical collar since. He is greatly missed, for we became very firm friends. He must have thought quite a lot of the cricket club for he left small legacies to Ernie Carey, Wally Tickner, Tony Geering and myself. Although he spent much of his time at the Sussex County Ground at Hove and also at Lords, he rarely missed a Sunday match at Barcombe and was always very interesting and entertaining company.

Albert and Jose came over for holidays again this year, bringing Albert's father and mother with them. Emil was not easy to entertain, but I had booked up for a week at Paignton, the same accommodation where Len and Janice had spent their honeymoon. The journey down was not very comfortable for the five of us packed tightly into Albert's VW Beetle was a bit of a squeeze. They enjoyed the country around Paignton and we managed plenty of sightseeing without travelling too far.

On our return to Barcombe, Emil was most anxious to visit Witney, the town he had been evacuated to during the First World War. (You will remember I mentioned this earlier in the book.) We spent a day there and he was delighted to find some of the people he went to school with, and this trip proved the highlight of the holiday for Emil.

Business methods began to change very rapidly during the sixties and it proved very worrying for small retail firms. Mergers were common and this often meant that many orders were transferred to the wholesalers. Although Mrs Elliott was now managing the business, one always felt that her heart was not in it.

We had persuaded Gilbert Hole to take over as president of the cricket club, but after a couple of seasons he had sold his farm at Culver and moved right away to Dorset. Tony Geering followed him as president but again after two seasons he sold up and moved down to Devon.

I had much fun with the 2nd XI. I found they did not take cricket so seriously as the 1st XI. After the match we would usually finish up at the Royal Oak. In those days, before the more recent alterations, there was a little bar between the Public and the Saloon called the Bottle & Jug. Four chairs either side with just enough space to reach the bar, and these were usually occupied by Geoff Collins, Arthur Blackman, Rufus Towner, Alan Stevens, Chris Wheeler, Bill Page and myself. Names to bring back memories of noisy hilarity and good natured leg pulling.

Len suffered a set back about this time. He had been troubled with his throat and chest, caused by the fumes inhaled by working in the broiler houses and on doctor's advice had to change his job. The firm had given him three months leave with pay but in the meantime he had to find other accommodation. Work was no problem to him and he immediately started with Woodgates, the milk delivery people. Where to live was the difficulty for he was on no council housing list and to find rented accommodation was almost an impossibility. He was advised to try to get a mortgage from East Grinstead Council and to his surprise they agreed to grant a mortgage for £2,400. They found a house at Ashurst Wood for £2,900, needing another £500 to reach this sum. However, the bank came to the rescue and agreed to finance him to this amount. Looking back, after many years, this move turned out for the best for it proved to be just the right time for buying a house. Soon after moving there Diane was born and Stephen was now old enough to start school.

It was about this time that the tennis club really got going. Roy and Pam Brook working hard to this end. The club was given a piece of land beyond the football pitch, large enough to house three courts, two of which were immediately put into use, with a third one following at a later date. Mr Faber and daughter, the local butchers, were the donors of this land.

We now had concentrated in this area, cricket, football, tennis, stoolball and bowls, plus the children's playground. Also the Primary School had use of the ground for physical training and sport. My dreams had come true and I wonder if anyone can name me another village in Sussex where all the sporting facilities are concentrated into one area.

1964 and a shock to my system. Not feeling well I had left work and retired to bed early afternoon. Brother George found me there and as it was so unusual for me to be ill, called the doctor. He arrived about five o'clock, took my temperature, prodded me about and then declared,

"Why, you've got appendicitis."

"Rubbish," I replied, "I don't even feel sick."

He chuckled and said, "Well, I'm getting you into hospital straight away, any preference?"

"Not Brighton General," I said, "Anywhere else will do."

Of course it was Brighton General. I arrived at about 7pm and by midnight I was minus one appendix and feeling as if I had been sawn in half and sewn together again.

I had no complaints about my treatment there. I think the nurses are wonderful but the hospital itself is so old and depressing. I was asked one day if I would like to go out on the verandah for a change of scenery.

"No thanks," I said, "Not to look at a lot of grey roofs, take me somewhere where I can see green fields and I will certainly say yes."

Eight days in hospital and I was ready for convalescence. Two sisters, Vi and Daisy King, very great friends of mine, had offered to have me for a week or so. They were living at Hurstpierpoint and a few days with them and I soon began the road to recovery. Len had also offered to have me, so after about ten days with the girls I went up to Ashurst Wood and stayed with Len, Janice and Stephen for another week or so. I recovered very quickly and was soon back at work and looking after myself.

Dr Hunter had bought the White Cottage near the parish church and he was elected the new president of the cricket club. Ernie Carey, the club chairman knew the doctor very well for he had been an excellent cricketer in his younger days and Ernie had met him on numerous occasions with the Sussex Martlets, the leading amateur cricket club in Sussex. The doctor always managed the Martlets tour to Cambridge University and Ernie for several seasons when up to umpire for them.

In 1968 came the upheaval of the first building development in the village. Place Farm, the old home farm of the Granthams, was sold to speculators. I remember the farm so well as a boy. I told you earlier of my visits to the dairy at Barcombe Place for a penny worth of skimmed milk every morning. I can still see that dairy with the huge flat pans of milk with the cream sitting on the top. How I longed to poke my fingers into it, but I never plucked up enough courage. The planning application came up before the parish council and there were some lengthy discussions on the issue. I remember an argument with Bill Webb, who expressed the view that it would ruin the look of the village coming in from the Newick Road. I recall saying,

"Come off it Bill, all you see now when you come over Clappers Bridge is a rough looking field covered in stinging nettles and brambles with a mass of dilapidated buildings at the top end, covered in rust and falling to pieces. I'm not in favour of the application, but not on those grounds. My objection is that I feel this is the thin end of the wedge, and very shortly we shall have over development for the size of the village."

However the application was granted, but twenty six years later and my fears have not been realised and we still remain a village to be envied, and Grantham Bank as the development was called has fitted well enough into the picture.

Another spell of important activity on the parish council. Mrs Anne Sants who lived at The Grange was in the chair at the time and she proved a very able and hard working officer. A planning application had been lodged to build fifty five houses on land between the garage owned by Brook and Churches and the now empty Barcombe railway station. At a parish meeting it was obvious that the majority present were against this proposal. I myself brought up the example of another village not far from Barcombe. When the station land was developed there the village people at the time thought it was a good idea and that they would get better train and bus services, a resident doctor, a chemist shop and generally better services all round. Much to the disappointment of the village, this did not happen and all they got was increased population without the extra services.

A petition was started and we attended in force a special meeting held in Lewes at which an administrator attended to hear views and assess the situation accordingly. We won the day and the appeal by the developers was turned down flat.

In the meantime a syndicate had purchased land to the west and north of the recreation ground in the hope that planning permission would be granted for the original proposition. Had this happened, no doubt in the years to come, the recreation ground would have been surrounded by development and even now this may eventually come, but thankfully not in my time. It wasn't all good news at this time for we lost our final rail link, the railway between Lewes and Uckfield closed, and although rumours often spring up, re-opening I fear is as far away as ever. My brother George was at Barcombe Mills Station for thirty six years until 'the end of the line', but moved up to a council estate in the village where he eventually died at the age of eighty.

Winter or summer at this time I was getting up to Ashurst Wood. Number three and the last of the children had arrived, another boy, David, and again I was invited to be godfather, so that meant I had some responsibility in bringing them up. Immediately on my arrival at Ashurst Wood, Stephen would be clamouring for me to take him to the local sports field with a ball and I had to spend many hours keeping goal for him. David also, as soon as he could walk, wanted no other toys if he could toddle around after a ball.

1968 and at the age of sixty I decided that I would retire from playing cricket. I remember when I had reached fifty I was determined to continue playing until I was sixty and that year I had a full season playing regularly and then called it a day.

The following year Len and Janice decided on moving. Six new houses were under construction at Plumpton Green, back home for Janice for her mother was still living there, and they managed to step in just in time to buy the last of these.

1969-1982

Although only seven miles to Plumpton Green, I found it very difficult to see them. It took me two hours by public transport, and although I complained to the Southdown bus company, I got no satisfaction. What was particularly annoying was the fact that the last bus from Plumpton missed the connection at Ditchling Corner, by about a minute, but they would do nothing to alter that. However, the situation was solved when a customer brought an item for the notice board. 'Raleigh Runabout For Sale'. "Do you think I could ride that?" I asked.

Being a middle aged woman her reply was, "Well, I'm sure if I can, you can!"

So I bought it and rode my first mechanised vehicle at the age of sixty. I found it took me just twenty minutes to get to Plumpton Green and I have been riding a moped ever since.

Twelve months later an official from the bus company called to see me to tell me they had altered the bus times to connect at Ditchling Corner. I must confess to getting a little pleasure from telling them what they could do with their bus service. I suppose it is not surprising that the rural bus services have deteriorated to be almost non-existent. It seems every family has one or more cars. So different to sixty years ago. A bus trip through the countryside was such a pleasure then and easily the best way to enjoy the passing seasons.

Stephen settled in well at his new school and proved very popular. He was very keen on football, but much to my disappointment I could not get him interested in cricket. David even at three years old showed great natural ability for all ball games.

1969 was a strange year for me. I was very tired and that was the excuse I invented to retire from everything. I did not seek re-election to the parish council and I had nothing to do with the cricket club. I could not keep interested in work and it didn't help that rumours were beginning to spread that Mrs Elliott had decided to sell the business. However, the rumours failed and it was 1971 before the business changed hands.

Although still continuing to umpire, Ernie Carey was suffering badly from arthritis and he was trying hard to get me to take an interest again in the cricket club. It was his suggestion that I should take up umpiring, but at that time I wanted to do nothing else but rest. I spent more time at

Plumpton with Len, Janice and the children, helping to get the garden up together, which was quite a job. I think the builders had left half their material behind under the ground. However, it began to take shape and today they have a garden which they are justly proud of.

Into the 1970s and Stephen started at the comprehensive school at Chailey. Diane and David were both at the primary at Plumpton and all three seemed to be doing very well. Len was working nearer home, as he had taken a job with a cooked meat firm, whose distribution centre was on Ditchling Common. Diane became interested in horses, and dad soon found her a pony to ride and a field to keep him in, and all her interest was centred on her pony. Velvet was his name and he was quite a handful to manage but Diane soon became boss and handled him very well.

1971 and the blow fell. Business had been very unsettled and the rumours became fact. The business was up for sale, and it wasn't long before a prospective buyer appeared. Mrs Elliott had informed us that he intended to keep all the staff on. So imagine our surprise and the blow to our ego, when the contract was signed, Miss June Trower and myself were not to be re-employed. June had for many years been in charge of the grocery department, doing all the buying, and I myself held the same position for the men's clothing and footwear, and the upstairs department of china, glass and hardware. I think we both thought we were indispensable, but as the new owner intended to do all the buying himself we were considered surplus to requirements. This left Mrs Elliott in the unpleasant position of having to give us both a week's notice, with tears and expressions of regret, and also meant she was responsible for finding our redundancy payments. For this situation I put the blame squarely on her solicitor for not having the promise of keeping all the staff on, put into writing.

I myself felt a bit like a fish out of water during the winter of 1971-1972, and we soon saw the shop completely altered and turned into a self-service, with the exception of the Post Office which, with Mrs Blackford in charge, still continued to give the service and help particularly to the old people, which they had experienced in the past.

During this winter, I took to visiting Ernie Carey once a week. He was suffering badly from his arthritis now and was in constant pain, but he never complained, and all he wanted to talk about was cricket. He continued to put pressure on me to take up umpiring and his enthusiasm was beginning to catch on, and I promised to seriously consider it when the season started.

Dr Hunter had proved an excellent choice for president of the cricket club and we had regular fixtures with St. George's Hospital of which the

Barcombe 1st XI, 1970

Back row; Jack Clarke, Colin West, James Stewart, Barry Wells, Brian Allsobrook, Richard Seager, Charles Seager.
Front row; John Osmond, Ian Newman, John Clarke, Dr I. Hunter (president), Keith Savage, David Trower.

Barcombe 1st XI, 1984

Back row; Martin Seager, Keith Burton, John Yallop, Barry Wells, Richard Seager, Gordon Wilkins.
Front row; Brian Allsobrook, Keith Savage, Ian Newman, Kelvin Spiers, David Peacock, John Osmond.

doctor was the dean. We were also playing Sussex Martlets, Sussex Doctors and St. Barts Hospital at this time.

1972 saw the introduction of the Haig Village Cricket Championship. This was open to any village in Great Britain with a population of not more than 2,500. The competition was divided into areas so travelling was no problem until after the area final. Our first match was with Lurgashaw in West Sussex and proved a most exciting game, Barcombe losing by just one run. Over the years since that first game, we have lost three other games by that single run, and have won one by the same margin.

Fund raising started in earnest for a new pavilion. Charles Seager put in a great deal of work in this direction and I am sure it was mainly due to his untiring efforts that the new building was erected in 1976. Grants were available but only for fifty per cent of the cost, so quite a large amount had to be raised and it took three or four years before sufficient cash was available.

I decided I couldn't just spend my retirement sitting on the seat at the bottom of the village. (I had instructed Geoff Trower, the local undertaker, to come and measure me up if he ever saw me there.) So I took on a few hours gardening at Galleybird Hall; and also a morning or so at Penance Pond, a delightful spot by the Parish Church. I found Mr Archer a very charming gentleman to work for and was very happy around there, providing his wife didn't interfere too much. A very unusual woman, so suspicious if anyone stopped and looked over the hedge, thought they were up to no good, rather than just admiring the lovely garden.

Another eventful holiday with Albert and Jose. I flew over as usual to Brussels and spent the first night at Albert's home. I was sent to bed early in readiness for a five o'clock start in the morning. I had no idea as usual where we were off to, but after about fifteen miles suddenly discovered I had left my passport back at Albert's place and had to return for that. We travelled all that day south through France, a boiling hot day, the sort of day when your shirt sticks to your back. It was late afternoon and Albert decided it was far enough for one day, so we booked into an hotel, freshened up, and enjoyed a pleasant evening and a good meal. The following morning we continued our journey and in the afternoon arrived in Andorra, high up in the Pyrenees and settled down for a week's stay there. There were masses of alpine flowers everywhere, but imagine my surprise the following morning when everything was covered with a couple of inches of snow. As soon as the sun got warmer it was wonderful to see all these flowers poking their heads through the snow. I have never seen so many different varieties in bloom at the same time. Many I know but lots of the alpines were new to me. Andorra is a most unusual place.

The one large town was at the time of our arrival just realising its potential as a tourist attraction and lots of new skyscraper hotels were in the process of construction. Getting about the country, we found lots of old ruins, completely dead villages; in such contrast to all the new buildings in course of erection. I think I enjoyed this holiday more, because of the wealth of floral beauty than for any other reason, for it was flowers everywhere at this time of the year.

Ernie Carey had at last managed to get me interested in umpiring at cricket. His arthritis was getting so bad now that he was practically a cripple. He persuaded me to do a game for Sussex Martlets at Lancing College as he didn't feel he could make the journey. He arranged that Alan Briggs, the resident umpire for the college, would meet me at Shoreham station and look after me, which he certainly did. A charming man, so dedicated to cricket and so sad that detached retinas in both eyes curtailed his enjoyment in the game at quite an early age. I thoroughly enjoyed the match in such beautiful surroundings and it was there that I suddenly realised how much I had missed mixing with younger people. Lancing College has been a favourite spot for me ever since that day. And so I was back again taking an active part in cricket, umpiring regularly both Saturdays and Sundays mixing again with younger people, and enjoying every minute of it.

The following year I was officially elected to the panel of umpires for Sussex Martlets and given a number of games to officiate at. I was also offered the mid-week matches for Hurstpierpoint College. Here I met and became friends with Derek Semmence and his charming wife, Christine. Derek was cricket coach at the college and although I finished umpiring several years ago, we still remain the firmest of friends and I regularly meet up with him when he is playing with the Sussex Over Fifties side, of which I am a keen supporter. I was also in demand for the Sussex schools and colts teams at all age groups from under eleven to under nineteen. I thoroughly enjoyed these youngsters' games for the skill and enthusiasm was of the highest order. The cricket ground at Hurstpierpoint is a delightful spot. Situated almost against the flint walls of the chapel, surrounded by trees, with a picturesque pavilion in one corner of the ground, in my opinion it comes a very good second to Arundel Castle. I find it very difficult to remember the boys from my early days of umpiring there, but often in later years I would come across someone who would greet me with, "I remember you from my school days at Hurstpierpoint."

In 1976 the new pavilion went up at Barcombe, and was much appreciated, particularly the toilets and showers, a very great improvement on the old facilities. Dr Hunter managed the Sussex Martlets tours to

Cambridge, and for a couple of seasons I had the opportunity of going with him as umpire. Four games were played Tuesday to Friday against Clare, Magdalen, Jesus and Emmanuel colleges. Lovely grounds, excellent accommodation and the opportunity to do a bit of sightseeing in this charming city. I met several Martlets members I had not come across before and found them excellent company. Dr Hunter also managed the Martlets side against the Sussex Young Cricketers, always played at Arundel Castle and I umpired this game for many years.

That year the club suffered the loss of Ernie Carey after a long and painful illness. I miss him very much, for during the winter months I was in the habit of paying him a visit on Wednesday afternoons for a cup of tea and 'cricket talk'. A hard working officer of the club for many years, he was sadly missed.

Stephen left school this year and started work for a firm of architects in Lewes. He was playing football for Plumpton now and a year or two later also at Barcombe where they had a Sunday XI. Diane was now at the Comprehensive at Chailey and the following year David followed her there.

1976 was one of the most successful years for Barcombe in the Haig Village Knock Out Competition. We won the Sussex Area, beating Fletching in the final. Sissinghurst of Kent were our next opponents, played at Barcombe. An excellent game, attracting a large crowd, but they proved too strong for us and we lost by seven wickets.

You will have to bear with me and my love of cricket for from now on to the end of my book it will take up quite a few pages. I had become a member of the Cricket Umpires Association, and this meant a few more games for me. I came across the following 'anon' poem which I found worthy of committing to memory and repeating on a few occasions at cricket dinners and functions. It always went down very well and I could usually introduce it as a 'leg pull' against one of the fast bowlers present. Entitled 'The Umpire', here goes:

Once upon a summer dreary,
While I wandered weak and weary,
Back towards my run up
After bowling hard for hours untold.
Though my fevered brow was streaming,
Still I wasn't idly dreaming
How to beat this stubborn batsman,
How to make the innings fold
'Ere the call of "over bowled".

In the light of this review
Of all the little tricks I knew of
Round the ball I wrapped my hand,
And subtly modified my hold.
Soon my effort was requited
As a slower ball well flighted
Dipped and hit the pads, delighted
"Umpire, how was that I called?"
Quoth the umpire, "Over bowled".

"That's a shame," I reasoned quietly,
I am disappointed, slightly,
Still, I must behave politely,
Mustn't let my wrath unfold.
He has given his decision,
Viewing from the best position,
My appeal got fair audition,
I must do as I am told.
Must accept his every judgment
Yes, must do as I am told
When he utters "Over bowled."

Next time round, I knew I'd got him,
Beat him playing back and caught him
Fair in front of middle stump.
An inswing in the 'Willis' mould,
Was appeal 'ere more compelling,
All the team joined in the yelling.
Round the ground it echoed swelling,
Sounded forth a hundredfold
Echoed in a great crescendo,
Amplified a hundredfold.
Quoth the umpire, "Over bowled."

"How was that," I cried astonished,
Fearing not I'd be admonished,
"That ball pitched on middle stump,
The track is flat and firmly rolled.
See his bat, he didn't flick it,
See his pads, he went to kick it.
Plus it would have hit the wicket,
That is all it needs, I'm told.
That exhausts the several tests,
That must be satisfied, I'm told."
Quoth the umpire, "Over bowled."

Thus enraged, two overs later,
Spurned by anger all the greater,
All three stumps I skittled down
With all the pace I'd known of old.
Up I leapt with gleeful cries of
Joy at conquest so decisive.
"How was that," I whined derisive,
This appeal you must uphold,
Here at last is an appeal
That any umpire must uphold.
Quoth the umpire, "No ball."

And the umpire ever grudging,
Isn't budging, isn't budging,
Though the teams are homeward trudging,
And the night grows dark and cold.
Still he stands, quite unashamed
Caring not how much he's blamed.
Still he'll stand, 'til God, who made
The laws with compasses of gold,
God above, ulterior umpire
Beckoning down from gates of gold
Will call him home with, "Over bowled."

    Easter 1977 and David started at Chailey, the comprehensive school. His sporting prowess had evidently preceded him for he was immediately made cricket captain of his age group, under twelve. However, through the staff being on a semi-strike, and refusing to do any out of school activities, David's cricket didn't make much progress.

    This annoyed me very much, for apart from the fact that Len and Janice had fitted him out with proper clothes and equipment, I knew he had enough talent to be worth encouragement. At the end of the summer, I suggested to Len that if I made him a junior member of the Sussex County Cricket Club, would they be prepared to get him down to the county ground at Hove on Saturday mornings for a series of coaching sessions. This they agreed to do and he duly arrived for the first of these, in the nets under the Gilligan Stand with Pat Cale the coach in charge of junior coaching in attendance.

    He quickly spotted David's ability and asked him where he played his cricket. David replied, "Nowhere! I only had one game at school as the teachers would not do out of school activities."

    Pat said, "Would you like to come and play with my team, Preston Nomads at Fulking."

And that was how David became involved, not only in the Preston Nomads side with Neil Lenham as his captain (now a professional on the Sussex staff), but also with the Sussex Schools and Sussex Colts at his age group. The following season he also captained the junior side at Barcombe and soon proved to have more than just average ability.

It was about this time that I became acquainted with Jack and Esme Woolley. It appears one Sunday they were out for a drive in the countryside and on stopping in the village street, heard the sound of ball on bat and so discovered the cricket ground with a match in progress. They took to visiting regularly and I very soon contacted them with a fixture card and a chat. Their son, Tony, was keen to play cricket and we managed to fit him in for a few games.

It wasn't long before they discovered the village, for they were fond of walking. Jack was just retired and they decided on buying a house in Barcombe, and finally settled on Stepney Farmhouse at the south end of the High Street.

We became very firm friends and have remained so over the years. they no longer live in Barcombe as they eventually found the house and garden too big, but they still continue to visit regularly. I look forward to their visits, for Jack has a ready wit and a comical sense of humour, but I manage to keep pace with him.

1979, and I got my first sight of Martin Speight. A game at Eastbourne between Sussex under eleven colts and Middlesex. As a ten year old he was very remarkable and his ability and self assurance was most impressive. I saw Pat Cale a few days after and told him I had seen a youngster who I thought showed great promise.

"Oh!" said Pat, "and who's that?"

"Martin Speight," I said.

"Don't worry, Sid, we have had our eyes on him for some time."

The next I hear of Martin, he had won a sports scholarship to Hurstpierpoint College and was now being regularly coached by Derek Semmence. I saw plenty of him later for he captained the side for his last couple of years there, and after going on to Durham University was taken on the Sussex staff and is now a regular member of the Sussex County XI. Derek Semmence proved a very popular coach at Hurstpierpoint College and no doubt his years of experience with both the county 1st and 2nd XIs played an important part in the success of the school in the realms of sport.

1980, and the Barcombe Cricket Club entered a league. Inevitable, for with league cricket flourishing all over the county, fixtures with other local sides were becoming increasingly difficult. We entered the Sussex

Championship League, which operated mainly along the coast between Brighton and Littlehampton. We never fully enjoyed these games, much preferring battles with local village sides, and some of the grounds we played on in the league left much to be desired. The spirit in which the games were played was also very different, but fortunately this situation was very short-lived, for by 1982 we had applied for admission to the East Sussex League and had been accepted. This meant we were back playing local villages such as Newick, Fletching, Ringmer and Glynde, which proved much more enjoyable.

Going back to the Championship League, I remember umpiring a game at Rottingdean. Their opening fast bowler became very aggressive towards me after I had turned down a series of appeals for lbw. I was not prepared to put up with abuse from him and after a word with the other umpire I informed the Rottingdean captain that if this aggression continued I should have to ask him to take this bowler off, and I would report the matter to the league management. He immediately stopped the offender bowling and after the game I received an apology from him.

"Sorry, Sid," he said, "We have had quite a bit of trouble with this chap. He is very aggressive, in fact he has been inside twice for assault."

I thought myself lucky all I got was mutterings and abuse.

Another umpiring incident about this time sticks clearly in my mind. Late in the season we had a friendly fixture away to Guestling, near Hastings. Whether it was the aftermath of a not very enjoyable league season, or perhaps the weather had got hold of them, I do remember it was a hot day, but the team behaved abominably. I gave a 'not out' decision against the opposing skipper for a catch behind the wicket, which our fellows thought was out, but for the rest of that game, the behaviour of our side made me very angry.

After the game, I got them all in the dressing room and tore them off a strip which I think they will all remember to this day. I finished off by saying, "Before I umpire another game for you, I will have a written apology signed by all the team."

I stalked out of their dressing room and into the home side to express my sincere regrets for the unforgivable behaviour of my team. The apology I had asked for arrived within the next ten minutes and I must say I have never had any trouble since. Recently I had a spell in hospital and Johnny Yallop (one of that team) came to see me. He recalled this incident with, "Crikey, you were angry that day. You made us all feel like little kids."

About this time, I was asked to umpire at Arundel Castle for the Duchess of Norfolk's XI, and I continued in this capacity for them for three seasons, until I eventually found it too difficult to get there and back on a Sunday. My first couple of seasons there my co-official was Vic Bruce from

Eastbourne, and when he discovered where I came from and how inconvenient it was to rely on public transport, he offered to pick me up in Lewes. This arrangement proved very satisfactory. However, Vic died suddenly from a heart attack at the age of fifty nine. What a shame, for he was such a charming man, and so popular with everyone at Arundel.

I had some excellent games there and looking through my lists I find fixtures such as Minor Counties South, Ireland, Scotland, MCC, Lloyds Bank among them. Colin Cowdrey often used to captain the eleven for the Duchess and many ex-county players turned up to play there. What a glorious spot! In my opinion it must be one of the prettiest grounds in the world and the arrangements there are so perfect it really is cricket at its best.

After Vic's death I had to back out of these games, but have continued to act as both umpire and scorer for Sussex Martlets whenever Charles Seager is officiating or David Peacock is playing.

David Peacock in action at Glynde, 1984

1982-1986

Wally Tickner died in 1982. He did so much for the Cricket Club in the early days after the war and would never accept a penny for his work. Barcombe owe much to him for the reputation we gained during the fifties, as one of the leading village clubs in Sussex.

Stephen continued to do well at work, now at Eastbourne where his firm moved to from Lewes. He passed his examinations and gained the letters B.I.A.T. after his name.

Diane was still pony mad and as she grew in size so did her ponies. Dad took her around to the shows and she did a bit of competition jumping.

Len again changed his job. His firm had moved down to the West Country, and as both Len and Janice were now firmly settled in Plumpton, and Janice's mother, who also lived there, was now getting frail, they were not prepared to move with them. He soon found work, a change from all previous occupations, as assistant caretaker at Chailey School.

David was now playing his cricket with Barcombe 1st XI and doing very well. The club had progressed well again this season in the Village Knock-Out Competition but had lost to Fletching, their old rivals, in the area final. David was chosen to captain the under sixteen Sussex Colts side to tour the West Country, and when Len rang me and said Janice and he intended to travel down to Cheltenham and spend the week under canvas, and would I like to join them, I didn't hesitate. They had a two bedroom tent and provided me with a camp bed, and I was quite comfortable, even though I was well over seventy by then.

David had an excellent week and handled his team with confidence. I thought his best performance was against Wales. In a low scoring game Wales were dismissed for 122 and the Sussex Boys lost nine wickets before passing this score, of which David had made 62 not out. The previous day he had made eighty against Somerset. The tour ended with a taste of the joys of camping, for on the Saturday morning it was raining hard and there wasn't much fun dismantling the tent and packing up, getting wet through in the process.

The Archers had decided on a move that year and Penance Pond was up for sale. It wasn't long on the market, and in October 1982 was purchased by Mr John Keffer. He asked me if I wanted to stay on and I agreed to do so for the time being to see how it worked out. In a very short while I had a key and was responsible for looking after the house while they were in London. Mr Keffer was still working and they were just spending the weekends here, from Thursday until Sunday evening. I had a free hand now in planning the garden and in no time at all it became 'Sid's Garden'. Although we had always had a couple of pairs of fancy ducks on the pond, Mr Keffer increased these to between thirty and forty, and these needed feeding twice a day. Having been pinioned as day old ducklings they couldn't fly, but this meant the property had to be completely netted to prevent their escape. They were quite colourful, particularly in the spring, and proved quite an attraction to visitors to the church.

I found Mr and Mrs Keffer delightful people to work for, so open and trusting, where the Archers were secretive and suspicious if anyone so much as stopped and looked over the hedge. The following spring and early summer when the garden was at its best, Mr Keffer took masses of photographs every weekend and soon had albums full of beautiful pictures.

David left school that year, Diane having left the year before and was working in Lewes in an office job. Although David had the opportunity to continue his education in the sixth form at Lewes, he did not think he would learn much more and wanted to go to work. Len had no objection, providing he found himself a job by the time school re-started in September, but on no account would he allow him to go on the dole. As no job had materialized by the start of the winter term it was back to school at Lewes for David. He hated it there and after three days, obtained an interview at the Technical College and although under the usual age of admission, was taken on for one term in accountancy. Between then and Christmas he saw an advert in the Evening Argus. 'Legal and General Insurance Co. have vacancies for three juniors', for which he applied and gained an interview to which Janice took him. He was smartly dressed and no doubt full of enthusiasm. On coming out his remark was, "Seventy applicants for three positions, and I don't think they were very impressed with me." However, forty eight hours later, a letter confirmed the job with 'Legal and General' was his, due to start the beginning of January.

1983 and another good run in the Village Knock-Out Competition. Reaching the final of the area and another meeting with our old rivals Glynde, and what a game. Barcombe made 151 for 8 wickets from their forty overs with 27 runs apiece from John Clarke, Richard Seager and Ian Newman. Glynde built up their score steadily and after thirty overs were 101 for 2 wickets. Then in the thirty first over David Peacock held two magnificent catches and changed the game, and Glynde were left needing 8 runs from the last over. After five balls four runs were needed from the last ball which was hit towards the long on boundary. A terrific diving stop by Richard Seager meant that Barcombe were the winners by 2 runs and into the last thirty two to meet Long Parish from Hampshire at Barcombe. A very strong side who had in previous years reached the final at Lords. Long Parish proved too good for Barcombe, but they could feel very proud of their performance that season.

Dr Hunter the club president had decided to retire and had bought a cottage in the High Street for himself and his sister to spend the rest of their days. "Sid," he had said to me, "When we move here in October I would like you to come along for coffee one morning each week, just to talk of nothing else but cricket."

Alas, it wasn't to be for the doctor suffered a fatal heart attack, while travelling on a London bus just weeks before his retirement. Such a loss to the cricket club for he had been an excellent president, and had intended to assist in coaching the youth side during the coming seasons.

The Keffers had settled in well and were looking forward to Christmas at Penance Pond. Their son Johnny was coming over from America, and I quickly realised that Christmas was going to be something special. The Christmas tree appeared, log fires were prepared for lighting and party invitations sent out for a real traditional English Christmas. Before coming to Barcombe, they had been spending weekends at a rented cottage at Plumpton and had already made several friends in the area. Everything went well and the only thing missing was the snow.

For the coming season David Hole was elected as president of the cricket club on Dr Hunter's death and John Osmond took over as chairman. The Trowers, David, who had acted as fixture secretary for many years and Paul who had taken over as captain of the 2nd XI proved very willing workers on the administrative side. Once again the club won the area final of the Village Competition. A long journey to Cople in Bedfordshire and again we were not good enough to progress further.

I was spending quite a lot of time at Penance Pond, but what a delightful place to be. So quiet, peaceful and relaxing, reminding me of my days in the choir so many years ago. We had a spot of bother with the ducks, eight disappearing completely in a fortnight and not a trace of them. I came to the conclusion it must be a fox, but meeting up with Capt Harding and his two Jack Russell terriers, which he took all round the pond, he declared no fox had been there; he was sure the dogs would have told him. However the game keeper at Conyboro, Fred Bayfield, was a friend of mine and I persuaded him to come along to see if he could discover the reason for the disappearances. He just walked around the pond, stopped under the willow tree, turned to me and said, "Sid you've got a mink. That's where your ducks have gone." He brought over a trap later, sent me off into Lewes to get some sprats for bait, and that afternoon I set up the trap. The following morning, there he was, the horrible looking beast, caught. I wonder if the crazy people who let these animals out of captivity realise the damage they do. We are only about half a mile from the Ouse, and along the stretch of river from Lewes to Isfield, all the moor hens and water voles have gone. They will also take pheasants, rabbits, chicken and anything else in the way of food that they come across. The only other time I have seen mink on the pond was the following summer. I had the boat on the pond at the time and one afternoon I suddenly spotted much disturbance of the water around it. I crept over to that side of the pond and peeped over the edge, and there were two young mink, about three quarters grown, chasing each other round and round the boat, and playing just like a couple of kittens. I managed to catch one of them the following day, but the other one just disappeared and I lost no more ducks.

1985. Stephen and Diane were both married that year. Stephen to Jenni and Diane to Malcolm. Both settled down in Hailsham, each buying a small property in the same road. Stephen was still working in Eastborne, so no great distance to travel, while Diane and Malcolm both worked for the same firm in Lewes.

David had been persuaded to play cricket in the County League for Littlehampton, though still playing for Barcombe on Sundays. I was a bit disappointed about this but I didn't try and persuade him otherwise, for he was old enough to make up his own mind. As his cricket was my number one priority I handed over the umpiring of the 1st XI to Don Hulks who was very keen and had recently joined the Umpires Association and I travelled with David to give him my support. Both David and myself were made very welcome with Littlehampton and Bill Lock and his lovely wife, Dawn, became very great friends of mine. Ian and Marge Murray, Ricky and Pauline Heberlein, Tony and Nicola Gammon and of course Brian Smith their wicket keeper from Ringmer, whom I had known for years all became friends of mine and have remained so ever since. It was Brian Smith's powers of persuasion that had decided David's decision to join them.

1986 and my brother George passed away after a long illness. He was well remembered by the local population for he was at Barcombe Mills station for thirty five years. Our local vicar was away and so unable to take the funeral, so we asked if it was possible to get the Rev. Webb, now living in Buxted to take it. He was approached and said he would very much like to do so. He drove down from Buxted, but was far from well, and suffered a minor heart attack on the way down. He had to be revived on arrival and helped into his clerical attire. When he started the service we thought it doubtful if he could continue, but as the service proceeded he seemed to regain his strength, and spoke sincerely of George as a friend.

1987-1993

February 1987 and Bill Webb also passed away. The funeral service was held at the Barcombe Parish Church which was filled to capacity. Although a very flamboyant character he was much loved in Barcombe and had made many friends all over the county.

It was a great surprise to me when I was asked if I would write a short article about Bill for the parish magazine. I agreed to do this on the condition that it was not altered in any way and the following is just how it appeared in the Barcombe News:

"I have fond memories of Rev. Webb from the first day he arrived in Barcombe. I had only recently been demobbed from the Army and was full of enthusiasm to restart life in the village where I was born, and to become fully involved in village life once more.

I found a kindred spirit in Bill Webb. His boundless energy and enthusiasm for all aspects of village life was endless. He immediately became interested in all the sports clubs. He played cricket at the time I was Captain of the club and enjoyed a game of snooker in the Men's Clubroom, and was particularly interested in all aspects of the Youth Sports and entertainments.

He soon became a member of the Parish Council, on which we served together for about fifteen years. At Council Meetings our opinions often differed greatly, and many a heated argument ensued, but this only made us firmer friends. His interest in the British Legion was well known all over the County, and members of the Legion from far and wide paid tribute at his funeral.

A keen supporter of the Fire Brigade. I remember well an Evensong at St. Francis - present were Wally Tickner, Les Churches, Bert Collins, Tom Pyne, Bert Anscombe, Arthur Hills and myself. Halfway through the sermon a message passed into the Church of a big fire at Handlye Farm and two whole rows of his congregation disappeared. A hurried finish to the service and Bill Webb had quickly joined us. A little sad that I am the only surviving member of that episode.

What a sense of humour. What a ready wit and above all what an entertaining personality. His command of language combined with an attractive voice made him a most interesting and clever speaker on any subject.

I am reminded of these words from Rudyard Kipling's poem, 'If':

> "If you can talk with crowds and keep your virtue
> Or walk with kings, nor lose the common touch
> If neither foes nor loving friends can hurt you
> If all men count with you but none too much."

To me that was Bill Webb. Not only our Rector, but a man I am proud to have called friend."

That year I was invited to become President of the Cricket Club in recognition of my services to the club in the past, a position I held for the next five years.

David had rejoined Barcombe and was made Captain. He had not been too happy playing County League cricket and also found the travelling from one end of the county to the other a bit wearying. He continued as captain for the next four years, but after moving to Ringmer where he had played football since a boy of fourteen, he decided to join them for his cricket. While playing for Barcombe he had scored twelve centuries, a record which will be difficult to pass.

October 1987 and the night of the hurricane. Not that I heard much of it in the night. My bungalow, being the middle one of three, is very sheltered from the wind. I certainly woke up a couple of times but did not realise the severity of the elements until venturing out next morning. Immediately I got on to the road it was broken branches and fallen trees everywhere. Within thirty yards one tree completely blocked the road to the village.

Already at eight o'clock in the morning a gang under the local tree surgeon, Brian Smith, was busy clearing roads from the village sufficiently to allow traffic to become mobile, and it wasn't long before it was once more possible to get in and out of the village. To ride my moped was out of the question and I decided to walk in some way to Penance Pond, to feed my ducks and view the 'ruins' I was sure my garden would be in. Three times on the journey there, I had to detour into the fields to bypass impassable fallen trees. Just before reaching Penance Pond I was faced by an impenetrable wall of fallen lime trees at Court House and it took me some time to clamber through the debris and finally reach my destination. Much to my amazement I found that although the road was completely blocked twenty yards either side of the house, the Parish Church seemed to have partly protected the trees in the garden. The roof of the church was badly damaged but Penance Pond was completely unharmed.

Some damage in the garden, one tree almost uprooted and leaning over the wall across the road. The Canadian maple by the church gate was just about split in half and the broken boughs landed in the pond. The ducks seemed little agitated, evidently far more able to deal with the elements than we are. I managed to contact Brian Smith the local tree surgeon fairly early and also was able to help out Miss Fletcher-Moulton, who was heartbroken over the damage around the Court House, for the trees that were down were all planted by herself and her companion, Dame Marjorie Maxse, years before.

With the help of two sisters, Margaret and Sheila Stewart, friends of Mrs Keffer, from America, staying at Penance Pond at the time, we were able to partly clear up the mess. On a later visit in 1993 they couldn't believe there were so little signs of the damage caused that night.

The following day, Brian Smith, turned up to clear the heavy boughs and trim the oaks, branches of which were twisted into unrecognisable shapes.

1988, I had decided, would be my last season as umpire. Hearing and eyesight are beginning to deteriorate and at eighty it's a long day on your feet.

I had a nostalgic last game at Hurstpierpoint College. Martlets against the Old Boys. A glorious day and a good game, but on the way home I managed to come off my moped, found some loose grit on the side of the road, out of control and over the handlebars and into the ditch. I must have been 'out' for about half an hour, for on coming round the first thing I heard was the siren of the ambulance. Quite shaky but I managed to ask the local Plumpton policeman to let Len and Janice know what had happened, and get Len to look after my bike.

I had expected to be on my way to Cuckfield but ended up at Lewes Victoria Hospital. After examination I was put to bed but woken up every hour for blood pressure and concussion tests. Next day I had X-rays and it was decided I should stay another night. In the meantime Len had trouble in finding out where they had taken me, and eventually had to get on to the ambulance service for that information. No broken bones, no concussion, and not even a bruise to show for my fall, and I was allowed home the following day. Len had dealt with the moped, and even that had suffered no damage.

David got himself married this year. He sold a flat he had purchased earlier at Seaford and bought a house at Ringmer. Lynne, his wife to be, although she came from Portslade, wanted to get married at Plumpton Church, but as the vicar would be away, they asked the Barcombe rector to perform the ceremony. The reception was held at Plumpton racecourse and attracted a great gathering of cricket and football enthusiasts.

I had taken to scoring, for my love of cricket was such I must be involved in some way to the end of my days. I came across another little gem from the umpire's pamphlet 'How's That', which I have committed to memory and bring out at cricket dinners, entitled,

'The Scorers Dream'

Some people dream of cottages, with roses round the door
While others dream of palaces, with servants by the score,
But I just dream of a scorebox with a carpet on the floor.

Some people dream of foreign climes, where bright hued parrots screech,
Of lazing in the sunshine on some sandy palm fringed beach,
But I just dream of a scorebox with numbers I can reach.

Some people dream of gardens, full of fruit and flowers fair
Where the lawn looks like a bowling green, and roses scent the air,
But I just dream of a scorebox with a comfortable chair.

Some people dream of sporting fame, for some athletic feat,
An Olympic gold, or an England Cap, to adorn the family seat,
But I just dream of a scorebox, with room to move my feet.

Some people dream of worldly wealth, the gold of old King Midas,
With cash enough to purchase cars and yachts, and planes and gliders,
But I just dream of a scorebox that isn't full of spiders.

Some people's dreams materialize, some never reach fruition,
But my dream of the perfect scorebox should be every club's ambition.

1990 was our last real effort in the Village Competition and again we reached the area final, only to fall to Fletching by one run. There is a particular reason why I have included details of this game in my book.

During the game I had pointed out to the local news reporter that Fletching had five brothers playing in their side. Father umpiring and mother scoring and that Barcombe had nine of their players actually born in the village, and didn't he think that was worthy of note. I thought that was truly village cricket, and one would have to travel a very long way to find a similar situation. His reply was, "Oh no, that's not news!" I suppose there was nothing sensational about it and the media and the press look for nothing else these days. So different from years ago when I can remember one read the newspapers to find out about the nicer things that were happening.

Last-ball drama as Fletching scamper home

THERE was high drama at Barcombe on Sunday as Fletching's last pair scampered a bye off the final ball to put them into the National Village Sussex final.

It was a nailbiting finish to a marvellous match in which fortunes fluctuated all afternoon.

Barcombe were 30-3 after 11 overs but a stand of 122 between David Peacock and Richard Seager revived the challenge. Seager's 50 came off 56 deliveries, while Peacock's 80 spanned only nine more.

That should have taken Barcombe past 200 but only 18 runs came in the last six overs, with Mike Elwin taking 4-8 in his last three to finish with 5-27.

Although that put the target within reach, Ian Newman's three spells cost only 14 runs and meant Fletching were always hard pushed to keep up with the required rate.

However, a second wicket stand of 94 between Mick Leeves and Mark Horscroft put them in a strong position before three wickets fell in quick succession.

It was then that Ali Horscroft joined his brother in a flourishing stand of 57 that left them needing only 18 off the last five overs.

But when Ali was bowled by Newman for a quickfire 31 that included two sixes and three fours, the pendulum again swung. Mark's dismissal, again bowled by the admirable Newman (5-14), produced panic and three were still required off the final over.

None came off Newman's first three deliveries and the fourth cost Guy Cogger his wicket. Elwin took two off the fifth to bring the scores level and that scrambled bye sealed a home tie against Staplefield on Sunday week.

For that they had to thank a combination of Elwin's bowling, some good fielding, Mark Horscroft's 87 off 75 balls and a total of 26 extras, including 12 leg byes and ten wides.

VILLAGE K-O SCOREBOARD

BARCOMBE
Savage c C Horscroft b Elwin 16
R Osmond c M H'croft b G H'croft ...2
Peacock lbw Elwin 80
Newman c Hoadley b G Horscroft 5
R Seager b Cogger 50
M Seager c AJ Horscroft b Elwin 7
Broadway b Elwin 11
Stewart c Leeves b Elwin 1
J Osmond run out 1
Tomsett not out 0
Extras 13
Total (for 9 wkts) 189

Fall of wkts: 1-11, 2-21, 3-30, 4-152, 5-172, 6-173, 7-177, 8-182, 9-189.

BOWLING: G Horscroft 9-1-28-2; Elwin 9-0-27-5; Jefford 9-1-44-0; Leeves 6-1-37-0; Cogger 7-0-40-1.

FLETCHING
Leeves c Newman b R Seager 26
AJ Horscroft c Stewart b Newman ..2
M Horscroft b Newman 87
G Horscroft b Newman 0
C Horscroft lbw M Seager 9
AB Horscroft b Newman 31
Cogger b Newman 7
Hoadley b R Seager 0
Jefford c Savage b R Seager 0
S Daniels not out 0
Elwin not out 2
Extras 26
Total (for 9 wkts) 190

Fall of wkts: 1-13, 2-107, 3-107, 4-119, 5-176, 6-183, 7-185, 8-185, 9-187.

BOWLING: Broadway 9-0-31-0; Newman 9-3-14-5; Yallop 5-0-31-0; M Seager 8-0-43-1; R Seager 9-1-55-3.

Sussex Express, 15th June, 1990

A couple of seasons after this game Barcombe were hosts to Crowhurst Park in a league match. The visitors arrived and it was obvious the skipper was in a foul mood. They fielded first and from the very start he was continually getting on to his team. Every dropped catch or misfield was an excuse for his annoyance, and everyone was getting fed up with his behaviour. After tea when Crowhurst Park went in to bat, wickets went down at regular intervals. After about the fifth wicket, the captain, who was batting, decided to change the batting order and called to the pavilion for so and so to come in next. The poor chap was not kitted up, and it took seven or eight minutes for him to prepare himself. The Barcombe side were getting a bit frustrated, and so were the umpires, and one enquired of the Barcombe captain if he wanted to appeal, to which on the spur of the moment he replied, "Yes." Whereupon the umpire met the player half way to the wicket and informed him he was out.

"Timed out," he explained. "By rules, you have only two minutes to reach the crease on the fall of a wicket." This infuriated the captain so much that he walked off declared the innings closed and gave Barcombe the points.

The local reporter was heard to remark, "This is too hot for me to handle. I'll get the Editor on to this."

Sure enough the following week's edition of the local press had an article by the editor on the sport page strongly criticising the sportsmanship of Barcombe. This upset the Barcombe players and they wanted to take the matter up with the press but were persuaded to leave it alone. The League management committee also discussed the matter, and came to the same conclusion, and so the incident was dropped. The only other repercussion came the following season when Barcombe met Crowhurst Park in the first league match, and were met by the chairman and captain of the club who apologised sincerely for last year's episode and hoped it would have no adverse bearing on the friendly relations between the two clubs.

Now that David was married and living in Ringmer I was not surprised when he decided to play his weekend cricket there. He knew so many of his age group, having played his football at Ringmer from the age of fifteen. As he was my no 1 priority where cricket was concerned I soon followed him on Saturdays and quickly became involved with the club, eventually being persuaded to do the scoring.

I soon got to know the boys well for I had met several of them from quite an early age through football. I made many friends; the Barnett family, the Crees family, Graham Pitts, Simon and Duncan Pugh, Mark Cherryman, Jamie Sykes, Terry Wheeler and many other players, supporters and officers of the club. I am sure there is no other sport that provides quite the same opportunity for friendships, and looking back over the years the numbers I have made must run into hundreds.

I had at last persuaded David to fill in application forms for membership to Sussex Martlets. It wasn't many years back when unless you were ex-college or ex-forces officer class you had little chance of being accepted. But things have changed and although a probation period is required it is now possible for anyone to become a member.

David was sponsored by Derek Semmence and Mark Allbrook of Hurstpierpoint College. He was lucky enough to get his first game at

Arundel Castle and this is how it came about.

I had scored a game there with Johnny Wills as manager and before leaving he asked if it was possible for me to score the following week there against the Free Foresters, a game which his father Geoff Wills was managing.

I said, "Sorry, no, unless Charles Seager is umpire, I cannot get down." Then I had a sudden thought. "If you can fit David Peacock, who is a prospective member, in to play, I could come with him and would be delighted to score."

Johnny's father lived in Jersey and he suggested I should telephone him the following day to see if he had completed his team. When I rang the next morning, Johnny had already been in touch with him and had persuaded him to fit David into the team.

So the following week we went to Arundel. I expect I was more nervous about the game than he was, for I would have been so disappointed if he didn't perform reasonably well, and on a nice day, which this certainly was, there are always quite a few spectators to watch.

The game kicked off with Free Foresters batting first and piling up the huge score of 270 for 0 wickets. When Sussex Martlets batted with fifty minutes batting before the tea interval, the openers only had 40 on the board with about five minutes to go before the break. The first wicket fell and David batted at number three, and after tea played a magnificent innings, scoring 109 without giving a chance, until he holed out to mid off through tiredness. The Martlets finished on 235 for 5 wickets, and I guess I must have been the proudest man at Arundel that day.

David was very much in demand for Sussex Martlets games the following season. Fortunately he worked flexi-hours which allowed him a certain time off, but even so he was unable to fit in all the games he was asked to play.

The following season, 1992, this was his average:
>Innings - 14;
>Not Out - 3;
>Runs - 910;
>Average - 82-7.

This included four centuries during the season. I was made an honorary member of the Martlets that year for services rendered over a period of more than twenty years. I always said the greatest service I had given them was to find them David Peacock. Anyway, I was delighted with the honour, for it isn't given lightly, in fact over the years I have been connected with the Club, I do not remember it happening before. I was invited as a guest to the Martlets Annual Dinner this year, held at the West Sussex Golf Club at Pulborough and I took David and Len along with me. A grand evening and such a delight to meet so many old members, some of whom I had not seen for years.

The first baby arrived in 1991 to Diane and Malcolm, a little girl, Samantha Jo. How quickly they grow out of the baby stage. She is now a proper little girl attending nursery school at three and growing up fast. The following year a little boy for Stephen and Jenni and he is now eighteen months old and getting about fast enough to cause upheaval in the home. When Jenni was expecting, Stephen unfortunately was made redundant, his firm more or less packing up altogether. He was out of work for several months, but eventually got taken on with a small family firm at Crowborough, where he is very happy and doing quite well.

David and Lynne started touring in 1989. A private cricket tour to Barbados, but as he did several tours between 1989 and the time of writing, I am devoting a chapter entirely to his visits overseas for cricket.

In the early nineties I became involved with the over fifties Sussex cricket team. Apart from one or two friendlies they played against Surrey, Kent, Hampshire and Essex in an all England Competition, the winners of the south east section going on to meet other districts in a knock out competition. The first year I went along as a supporter, Ken Suttle, the old Sussex county player, was the captain of the side, but he had to retire for medical reasons and Bill Lock took over as captain the following season.

Brian Smith from Ringmer was still keeping wicket (now in his sixties) and he would pick me up from home for these matches. I enjoyed these trips very much for the games were usually played on the county crounds such as Southampton and Gravesend. The teams often had an ex-county player or two included and it was a pleasure for me to find names that I knew of when I was in my prime, and to find the standard of the 'old 'uns' so high.

My president's game was a great success again this year, six of my old Littlehampton friends turning up to play for me, bringing their families with them and enjoying a picnic on our lovely Barcombe ground. Old friends like Jack and Esme Wooley, and Cyril and Jean Tasker always came to these games and Frank Farrell always umpired for me.

Into the nineties and I had persuaded the Barcombe Cricket Club to allow me to retire as President. I wanted Charles Seager to be elected in my place, for he had worked so hard for the club for many years.

David was another reason for my wishing to retire. For some time now he was my No. 1 priority where cricket was concerned, and if he was playing for Ringmer, or all over the county for Sussex Martlets, he would always come and get me and I no longer felt very confident about travelling on my own. Charles Seager was also very good for he had many games umpiring for Sussex Martlets, Sussex Schools and Sussex Young Cricketers.

I usually scored in these games, so it meant I was still very much involved in cricket.

In 1992, on my 84th birthday, Mr and Mrs Keffer presented me with a magnificent album of photographs of 'My Garden' at Penance Pond. Beautiful pictures of the seasons starting with snow scenes early in the year, then going on through spring, summer, autumn and on to winter again. This has given me much joy, not only to look through on rainy cold days but to show to friends and visitors on every possible occasion. All of the pictures are taken by Mr or Mrs Keffer (both keen amateur photographers) and much careful thought must have gone into the selection and presentation of this wonderful book.

I really began to feel my age for I was in constant pain with my right leg and back. Eventually I saw my doctor, and after X-rays and visits to a specialist it was decided I needed a hip replacement and I was put on the list for an operation, estimated waiting time about a year. I found it necessary to use a walking stick now and most gardening was with the help of a kneeling stool.

I was lucky enough to persuade Miss June Trower (who I had worked with years ago at the shop) to spend a couple of afternoons with me in the garden, or if wet working in the house. This proved a huge success for she had previous experience of garden work and could turn her hand to any job.

My leg became progressively more painful both day and night and after twelve months I again got in touch with the Sussex County Hospital but they could give me little hope of an early operation.

I went to Jersey in April of 1993 for a weekend with the over fifties Sussex cricket team, who had arranged a couple of games there, one against the local college and the other against the Jersey over fifties side. Although I found it very tiring, I enjoyed it very much. Fortunately the companion I travelled with looked after me very well and immediately on our arrival in Jersey we were able to hire a car to get us about, otherwise I should have been such a nuisance. It was a delightful break and I enjoyed every minute of it. The island in April is most beautiful and spring comes to them much earlier. I was so tired on my return I spent the next twenty four hours between the sheets.

A new pavilion was built that year, incorporating the bowls club, storage and equipment facilities all in one building.

Brian Allsobrook, with his sponsored London Marathon walk raised £1,400, a magnificent effort from one individual. Grants were available from several sources and were much easier to obtain then in the past.

Penance Pond, Barcombe, in the spring of 1986

September and the date draws near for my admission to hospital. Len and Janice were most helpful in getting me ready and Janice took me to the Princess Royal Hospital on the fourteenth and waited with me until I was documented and settled in. A charming nurse took my particulars and she was highly amused when I replied to her question "Was I allergic to anything" with "Yes, women". No time lost, the operation the following day and I remember little for the next forty eight hours. Janice and Len came in to see me regularly and dealt with everything that was necessary.

They have been so good to me, I would have been most unhappy without their support.

After the first two or three days get well cards and visitors were arriving very regularly. I didn't know I had so many friends.

It wasn't long before I was getting around with first the aid of a zimmer and then with crutches. What I found so amazing was the fact that apart from the discomfort of the operation, the pain from my hip had completely disappeared.

Mrs Patricia Hill had recently undergone a similar operation, and some time back had offered to have me for a week or two's convalescence at her home at Mount Pleasant. She came to visit me in hospital and renewed her invitation, which I decided to accept.

One surprise visitor was Lynne, David's 'ex', whom I was very pleased to see for I had become very fond of her. It was a sad meeting, for I fear there is little chance of them getting back together. A further unwelcome setback in hospital for my waterworks went wrong and I was fitted up with a catheter. This meant a few extra days in hospital before I was fit for discharge. I could not get used to hospital food, but otherwise I could not fault my treatment, and I saw many people there who were much worse off than myself, and I have the greatest admiration for the nurses and staff who do such a wonderful job.

I had decided to write my memoirs and got started the very first day of my admittance. Eighty six years in one village might make interesting reading, and even if they never see publication, they would at least give me an interest over the coming winter, and possibly keep me from complete boredom.

Four or five of David's cricketing friends from Ringmer turned up one evening. I thought they might be a bit rowdy, but they were on their best behaviour and caused me no embarrassment. Steve Barnett the Ringmer skipper and his charming wife Julie turned up a couple of times. They live in Haywards Heath and it was nice to see them. Mr and Mrs Keffer also paid me a couple of visits. So many visitors made the time go quickly and the end of my three weeks stay at the hospital was soon over.

One special visit I must mention. My niece Margaret brought my dear old friend from Southwick, Miss Vi King to see me. Now 92 years old and still going strong.

I soon settled in with Patricia Hill, my charming hostess and 'nurse' and her son Nigel. Apart from getting out walking up and down the road with the aid of a couple of sticks, I spent practically all day in her lovely sun room, with its wonderful views of the village and beyond it to the South Downs. It also provided a golden opportunity to get on with my book, and I am sure the pleasant surroundings were a source of inspiration.

Back home about the middle of October. I had persuaded Clare Ridley to come in once a week to clean up the bungalow, and the Home Help Service were providing me with a woman to call in every morning just to light my fire. I was getting on well enough walking, and had managed about a mile every day, when I went down with a chest infection. A week in the Lewes Victoria Hospital on antibiotics and I felt much worse than I had while in the hospital at Haywards Heath.

Then in November I had a sudden telephone call from the Princess Royal Hospital. "Could I turn up on Monday for admittance for my prostate operation." I simply replied, "Yes, please," hoping to get everything over before Christmas and regain my strength before the spring arrived. However it was not to be for here we are at the end of April and I'm still lacking in energy and cannot get about more than a few yards without the aid of sticks.

David's Overseas Tours
1990-1991-1992-1993

David's first trip abroad for cricket was to Barbados. More of a holiday than a cricket tour this one, for Lynne went with him and cricket was limited to three or four games. Ian Newman was also on this tour and I think they had a very enjoyable time.

During the summer of 1990 David got to know an eccentric character, Michael Wingfield-Digby, who was the organizer for the Cavaliers Cricket Club (an offspring of the Christians in Sport movement, a body which boasted members from all branches of sport), and he was invited to tour The Gambia the following January. Apart from playing three one day limited overs matches, and two two day test matches the tour members undertook regular coaching sessions at the schools.

David agreed to go taking Lynne with him for another cricketing holiday. The tour was a huge success and a most enjoyable one for both David and Lynne, for they knew several of the tour members quite well. Martin Hole was a member of the Barcombe Club and Charlie Hartridge of Lewes Priory, plus John Bushel and his son Neil which made the trip a very pleasant one right from the start.

I had persuaded them to keep a diary for me and of course I find this very useful now. David did particularly well and in one of the two day tests scored 162 runs, the highest ever for a Cavaliers player. He also made himself very popular with the local lads, coaching them in both cricket and football. One or two of the places they played at were a bit primitive, but they thoroughly enjoyed themselves and came back very brown.

I had thought that Lynne might be a little bored with David playing so much cricket but she was a very avid reader and as long as she had a book and could soak up the sun in January she was perfectly happy.

David was such a hit with the local boys. There were always three or four waiting outside his hotel to carry his bags. He bought them a football and was much in demand to play with them any spare moments he had.

David's next trip was to Zimbabwe, November 1991 with the Sussex Martlets team, skippered and managed by John Bushel. A very ambitious tour this, for apart from South Africa, Zimbabwe were the strongest of the African countries cricketwise. They landed at Harare Airport at 6.20 am after a ten hour flight and met up with their hosts. David and Lynne stayed with a past chairman of the Stragglers Cricket Club in a huge bungalow with lots of land, a swimming pool and a couple of servants. David wrote "I could easily get used to this".

Later they went off to view the local ground (where John Major recently played) and for a welcome party with their hosts, before retiring early, as both were very tired. The following morning a couple of hours in the nets in preparation for the opening game next day. John, Neil, Keith Jenkin (also on the previous tour with the Cavaliers to The Gambia) picked the team. David wrote, "Our first game was against South Harare, who batted first. Mark Semmence (son of Derek of Hurstpierpoint College) bowled well and took the last three wickets in four balls and they were all out for 183. We batted slowly and when I went in at number 6 we needed 75 at over five an over. I got 41 not out in a partnership with Neil and we won quite easily."

Again, from David's diary, "The next day to Trelawny, about an hour's journey from Harare. This is the club where Graham Hick started and we met his parents. another nice ground where we waited for our hosts to pick us up. We are staying with a tobacco farmer in a massive house. He has a 'few' Mercedes, several dogs, masses of land and two small airplanes in the back garden. He and his girl friend can both fly and plan to take Lynne up while we are here but I am going nowhere near, I hate flying.

There is still a big class difference here. Everywhere we have been there are black servants, waiters, gardeners and golf caddies. In some ways it is very sad.

The next day cricket on a wet bouncy wicket after overnight rain. I opened the innings and after scoring four, I was hit full in the face from a ball which lifted off a length. I was rushed off to a doctor who X-rayed me and treated me for shock and concussion. I had an injection and was given more tablets to take to go with my nice swollen face and black eye. Trelawny won this game by two wickets."

Two or three more games near Harare and a visit to a game park and then they flew to Bulawayo for two games of cricket and the gem of the tour, the visit to Victoria Falls. After the first game there a free day for sightseeing, Lynne went on 'The Flight of the Angels', a helicopter trip over the falls. David couldn't be persuaded to try that one and instead went white water rafting which he described as terrifying but absolutely fantastic.

They returned to Harare two days later and the night before leaving for home the Martlets hosted a party for the friends they had made and a most successful tour ended with honours even, for they had won three, lost three and drawn one.

February 1992 and the Cavaliers third tour to The Gambia and the second one for David. They again had several sessions at the schools, coaching with the boys but were disappointed that the standard of their cricket had not improved. David soon met up with several of the boys he got to know on the previous tour and again proved very popular with them.

Jim and Jenny Hastwell and their son Matthew were on this tour. Matthew I had got to know very well at Hurstpierpoint as a schoolboy and a prominent member of the 1st XI cricket team. Jim Hastwell was the Vicar of Forest Row and he and his wife were very charming people.

David scored plenty of runs during the tour but was disappointed that the opposition was not stronger. He had one score of 99 and finished with an average of 62-5. Plenty of golf, swimming and lazing around the pool, combined with the evenings spent in the company of the tour personnel made it a wonderful holiday again, but not so good from the point of view of cricket.

The Cavaliers Tour to Uganda, 1st to 23rd February 1993. David is on his own for this tour, he and Lynne having 'split up' in October of last year. I am particularly sorry about this, for over the years I had grown very fond of Lynne.

The trip to Uganda is a very ambitious one for the Cavaliers, for Uganda is considered the strongest of the African Nations apart from South Africa. Ten of the party have travelled with the Cavaliers on previous tours and with Tim O'Gorman, now with Derbyshire and previously Durham University, and Graham Harding, Tim's skipper at Durham, plus Richard Davies, the coach at Lancing College, the team was of reasonable strength.

A brief stop at Nairobi, Kenya, then off to Entebbe. David is staying with Cephus Taylor and Richard Davies at a massive house with their hosts Abbey and Carrie, who proved great fun.

A reception in the evening of the first day meeting all their hosts and filmed by Uganda T.V. The following day a 20 overs game with a local school and then a session of coaching with the boys. David writes, "It is very green and lush here and lots of grass because of lots of rain. Everywhere very beautiful. There is much poverty, but not starvation as so much grows. The boys were good and very, very keen. I got so much from these kids. The enjoyment they get from such simple things makes me feel so humble."

The following day another coaching session with the schools and in the evening a cocktail party with the High Commissioner.

Then came the visit of the Pope. Thousands turned out to see him and the tour party had a day off from cricket. Down to Entebbe and Lake Victoria and eight of the party, including David, went fishing in boats for Nile Perch. They are very big fish and David caught one which weighed ninety two pounds. When I asked "What did you do with it?" his answer was "Took it to the Salvation Army."

Apart from the cricket, the standard of which was very good, they had plenty of opportunity for sightseeing. The source of the Nile and the Mountains of the Moon were very beautiful and spectacular.

A trip up country to a place called Fort Portal, high up in the mountains. Saw plenty of wild life on the way up, Impali, warthogs, and massive baboons. The following day on a game drive there were lions, hippo and buffalo, etc. David describes the lodge where they stayed as the most beautiful place he had every seen.

He was again proving very popular with the boys. The first evening here he organized a proper football match against the locals, eleven of them against eleven of the tour, with proper referee and linesmen and well over a hundred spectators. Result, one all and David got the goal for his side. The locals called him 'Maradona'. After the game they all went back to their camp, sang songs around the campfire, drank some of the local home brew which was very strong. David describes this as the highlight of the tour so far.

The following day back to Kampala. The driver of the landrover was ill with malaria so David drove, a six hour journey which made the time go much quicker for him.

The last game of cricket against the 'White Caps', a grand finish to the tour, for it finished with the 'White Caps' needing ten off the last over to win. They got three singles, a six and needed one off the last ball which they got and won the game.

David's hosts had asked him back for Christmas and he was also approached by their sports representative and minister to go back for a month to coach their youngsters in cricket and football as he had proved so popular with them. And so back home and start planning for the next tour. The Cavaliers plan to visit St. Lawrence in the West Indies in January 1995.

David also went on two weekend trips to Paris to play the sporting club there. On each trip he managed to make a century and this year the fixture is in August and he is helping to organize it.

1994

After a lapse of four years Barcombe Cricket Club have a team in the National Village Cricket Championship again.

In the first round they were drawn away to Selmeston, who were unable to raise a team for this fixture, so Barcombe went through to the next round by default. This meant a match against their old rivals Glynde, whom they had met on more than one occasion in the final of the Sussex area.

Barcombe had the advantage of a home fixture and also won the toss and decided to bat. Not a very good start for two wickets were down for twenty five runs, but a partnership of ninety between Sanjay Patel (76) and Richard Seager (38) put Barcombe in a strong position. 20 from Martin Seager and then a very quick 45 from Ian Newman, with four consecutive sixes landing over the hedge into the garden at Hillside, and Barcombe finished their forty overs at 227 for 9 wickets. Glynde were always struggling to keep up with the run rate and although their captain, Hurrell, made an excellent 73, part of the time batting under difficulties with a runner, were all out for 141 in thirty seven overs. Stewart Still, 3 for 33, Ian Newman, 2 for 18 in seven overs and Paul Coppard, 2 for 29, all bowled well.

Away to Ditchling for the next round, Barcombe lost the toss and were put in to bat on a slow wet wicket and a slower, wetter outfield. Runs were difficult to come by. Four wickets down for 53 wasn't very good but with Patel (46) joined by Paul Coppard (37) a useful partnership took the score to just on the hundred. Barcombe were all out for 153 in the fortieth over which, considering the slowness of wicket and outfield, I considered a creditable performance.

Ditchling were always struggling and apart from a partnership of 60 for the seventh wicket between Matthew Searle and G. King, were dismissed for 118 in the thirty ninth over. Ian Newman, 2 for 14, Stewart Still, 4 for 30 and Paul Coppard, 2 for 30. Paul Coppard has improved greatly over the part two seasons and is one of the best all rounders in the club today.

Our next opponents were Poynings, a team we had met twice before in this competition. The fixture was fortunately at Barcombe for I know our team would not be happy on the Poynings ground. We again won the toss and elected to bat. Keith Savage was out for seven. He had not yet returned to form after missing the whole of last season with a broken leg.

A partnership of 101 between Sanjay Patel and Stewart Still set things well on the way to a big score. Still went for 51 but Patel carried on to a brilliant century, being unbeaten on 102 after forty overs. Ian Newman (31) and Paul Coppard (22 not out) helped the score along to 244 for four wickets.

Poynings were never in the hunt and were all out for 135. Stewart Still with 4 for 17, Richard Seager, 3 for 43 and a tidy spell from Keith Hunter 1 for 31 in nine overs, plus seven overs from Ian Newman producing only fifteen runs. The fielding seems to improve with every game and I'm sure has much to do with our success.

This win put us into the final of the Sussex Area and another meeting with our old rivals, Fletching. We have met three times before in the final and have lost every time to them by a very close margin, the last time by just one run. Again, we had the advantage of home ground but not the luck of the toss which Fletching won and elected to bat. A couple of wickets fell cheaply, but a partnership of just on a hundred took the score to 158 for four wickets after thirty three overs. Our bowlers stuck to their task well and Fletching were finally all out for 202 in the fortieth over. Mick Leaves made an excellent 77 and Grant Horscroft with 39 gave able support.

Barcombe started badly and had lost three wickets for only 27 runs. Then Richard Seager (46) and Keith Savage (82) rescued Barcombe with a stand of over 100 with some excellent forceful batting. A lively innings of 25 from Paul Coppard and a four from the last ball of the forty overs saw Barcombe home. Again, the fielding was of a very high standard and seems to improve with every game. This I am sure had had a great influence on our successful run in this competition.

A wait of a day or so to find our opponents in the next round were Goatacre, Wiltshire, unfortunately an away fixture, against a side which had won the Championship on two previous occasions, 1988 and 1990. Two coach loads and several cars travelled up to Wiltshire to ensure we had plenty of supporters to cheer them on. A glorious day and arrived at the ground in good time. A small pretty ground, so small no cars allowed and only just room for a single row of chairs outside the boundary rope. The ground was so enclosed it seemed even smaller than it was.

The clubhouse pavilion acted as the village centre for it boasted no single shop or public house and the population was only a little over 200. An airfield quite near evidently provided them with some of their players. Their captain, Iles, had made a century in the final at Lords in 1990 and we were soon to discover that he was more than the mainstay for their team.

Goatacre won the toss and elected to bat and after twenty overs we seemed to be doing well for we had three of their wickets down for only 63. Then in came Iles who treated us to a spate of big hitting, the like of which

I certainly had never seen before. He scored 112 which included eleven sixes and seven fours. The Barcombe fielding was of a very high standard and all possible catches held but there isn't much you can do to stop sixes. The innings closed at 258 for 8, a colossal score for forty overs even on such a small ground. Ian Newman taking 4 for 48 and Keith Hunter, 2 for 35.

Facing this mammoth task, Barcombe started briskly but lost the first wicket at 25, Stephen Heasman bowled round his legs for 15. A good partnership between Sanjay Patel (40) and Keith Savage (60) took the score to just on 100 after twenty overs. Stewart Still fell to a debatable catch on the boundary without scoring and in came Richard Seager. Evidently Dick's mood was "Anything you can do, I can do better." for he proceeded to hit seven tremendous sixes, all of them further and higher than those hit by Iles. Unfortunately he was bowled on 49 with the score at 190 and seven overs to go.

Paul Coppard tried manfully to carry on the good work and made a spirited 29 before being caught one handed on the long on boundary. A brilliant catch which would have been a certain six.

Our innings closed at 232 in the fortieth over and everyone thought we had nothing to be ashamed of with a performance like that. Our fielding in particular was of such a high standard it could so easily have won us the game.

And so it is wait for 1995 to see if we can improve on our results and perhaps even get to Lords for the final. With our success this season we have great hopes that this is possible and look forward to the opportunity to prove it.

September again and the end of another cricket season and also the end of my book. The season has seemed so short, the weather interfering all through May and again this month, that really we have only had June, July and August to enjoy my favourite sport. Football also encroaches into the season more and more and soon will be played from January to December. Not in my time I hope.

I have not yet regained my strength and am still walking with a couple of sticks but I am hanging on to the moped for the winter in the hope that by the spring of 1995 I might feel strong enough to once more get around on it. I still intend to live to be one hundred, perhaps I might even write another book!

Barcombe 1st XI, 1994. Team final, village KO competition.
Back row; Richard Seager, Martin Seager, Ian Newman, Stephen Heasman, Chris Tucker, Richard Osmond.
Front row; Keith Savage, Keith Hunter, Paul Coppard, Stewart Still (capt.), Andrew Allsobrook, Sanjay Patel.